I0188305

ON THE
BACK BURNER

The Conversations We Should Be Having

LEE STOERZINGER

Copyright © 2015 Lee Stoerzinger

All rights reserved. No part of this book may be used
or reproduced in any manner whatsoever without
prior written consent of the publisher, except in the
case of brief quotations embodied in critical articles
and reviews. Special book excerpts or customized
printings can be created to fit specific needs.

For more information contact:
Lee Stoerzinger
lee@leestoerzinger.com

ISBN Numbers:
Hardcover: 978-0-692-48669-6
eBook: 978-0-692-48670-2
Library of Congress Control Number: 2015946043

Securities and advisory services offered through SII Investments, Inc.
Member FINRA/SIPC and registered investment advisor.
Lee Stoerzinger, Inc. and SII are separate companies.

This book was written with technical assistance from
BusinessGhost, Inc.

This book is dedicated to my wife and children.

*Maggie, who taught me that sometimes in life,
doing things "the fun way" is better than "my way."*

*And to my beautiful children,
who helped me realize that it's never too early
in the morning to DANCE.*

CONTENTS

Preface

From the Heart

THANK YOU for taking the time to open this book. It means more to me than you will ever know.

The following chapters may be different from what you expect, and unlike anything you have ever read. This is not a self-help program or "six steps" to anything. Nor is it a book on financial planning or investment advice.

If I had to describe it in its truest sense, I would say it is a hopeful beginning to a conversation about who we are as a people and what we want our present moments to look like. It is a collection of ideas, facts, stories, and inspirations, all relating to the reality of the world we live in. Music has the ability to conjure up strong emotions. Since I am not a good singer, I hope these written words will carry a tune into your heart and mind.

"On the back burner" is a metaphor for something I have been thinking about for a long time. The approach is simple;

our values tell us certain things are important: family, community, or faith, for example. It is my contention that, at this point in our social evolution, many of the things we claim to hold dear have been moved to the back burner of our lives. There's a disconnect between what we honor and the ways we are really living.

This is the hypothesis I want to explore with you. And while I do not claim to have the absolute answers, it is my aim to start the conversation.

For more than two decades, I have had the blessing of doing what I love in my work. My title is CERTIFIED FINANCIAL PLANNER™ PROFESSIONAL. Wait, don't close the book yet! I promise I'm not going to sell you anything. Be honest. When you hear those words, what do you think of? Someone who brings you investment pamphlets or wants to discuss insurance? A person in a suit who sits you down to fashion a long-term plan for living in retirement? I have never really viewed it that way.

Here's another question: What are the most important priorities in your life? I feel that the true depth of my job is helping people identify those most important things and define what they truly mean. Moreover, I teach people how money works in their lives, and blend the two together. In my mind, that's what a true financial planning professional does.

Long-term experience in the financial service business has given me a unique perspective. First, we financial planners share in the most intimate parts of people's lives—births, weddings, work achievements, and even sickness, loss, and death. Second, we are firmly planted at the epicenter of the modern world: money. Money cuts to the emotional roots of every human issue. But in my years of advising, I've come to understand that when we talk about money, we're layering in fear, spirit, and soul. Nothing is more important in my occupation than trust, and I am proud to earn the confidence of the people I work with, work for. We connect on a level far deeper than dollars and cents.

So when we talk about money, let's be honest—we're not really talking about money.

Each of us is a culmination of past experiences, culture, family history, etc. We are all trying to get by, do what is right, and live the best lives possible. We are presented with great opportunities and tough roads along the way. I spend my days meeting with people and learning about the unique experiences that make them who they are. We help them set and meet goals, sending them off into the sunset, so to speak. We are grateful to have each of them in our lives.

Until recently, I thought that the processes we'd developed to secure solid, long-term relationships were as good as they could possibly be. After all, our clients were very happy with us, and we were thriving as a firm. We saw the tangible proof that we were improving people's lives. We prided ourselves on integrity and proactive strategies. We were hitting all of the markers, so to speak. However, as our relationships grew, I saw patterns that unsettled me. The faces were different, but the stories were the same.

For example, I started to see how hard it is for parents to talk to their children about their finances. Why is it easier to follow the markets than our financial plans? Why are faith and participation in community in such steep decline? Families today are exhausted and torn apart, and they don't even know what they are chasing. Still, they stay on the treadmill. What are they looking for? Why do we take our aging parents miles out of their comfort zones to end their lives in "nursing homes?" Is it because our own lives are so busy that we are unable (or unwilling) to care for them? We nod our heads and admit that these are important issues, but we fail to do anything about them. It saddens me that we don't step back and refocus. We build our lives into a clean box that looks great on paper, justifies our actions, and maybe even tells a good story. Yet we fail to honor the things that we claim to be committed to, which in reality are the foundations of our lives.

In our firm, we had all the right tools, people, and processes to address the planning side of these topics. But the "real stuff" seemed to fit in at a lower level, and we acknowledged that we had to look to the root of these problems. I didn't want to tiptoe around the proverbial elephant in the room any longer, so I gathered my courage and posed some serious questions—to my clients, my staff, my family, my friends, and most important, to myself. Once I broke from the safety of the status quo, my mission became clear and my life changed forever.

It was February 14th, 2010—Valentine's Day. My wife, Maggie, and I were leaving church on our way to a special brunch, and I noticed her talking to a friend. I joined them and heard the friend say, "There are several families who are adopting children from Haiti, and you are going to do it with us." This was right after the devastating earthquake that killed 300,000 people—the one we all heard about on the news. My wife and I laughed nervously as we worked our way out of the conversation.

A short time later, comfortably seated at brunch, something real and emotional came over us. Our hearts were still back in the church conversation. It was very, very powerful. We looked at one another and thought to ourselves, why not? We ate our food as quickly as possible and rushed back to join "coffee and doughnut" Sunday. We joined several other families who were gathered in the church basement. I remember papers being passed around, and talk about children. We were eager to learn. A group of about thirty children needed homes. They were staying in an orphanage at the Missionaries of Charity in Port Au Prince—Mother Teresa's Sisters.

After much discussion, we dove in. There were letter requirements, applications, and a daunting pile of paperwork. They were trying to rescue as many children as possible, but the government system was in shambles—an already weak nation disabled further by a natural disaster. Buildings had been destroyed, records lost, and human lives evaporated. Maggie and I realized the overwhelming state of despair, tragedy, and need. It was hard enough, from our end in the northern United States. What were we getting into?

A few weeks later, we received a call. It was the head Sister of the Caribbean region. She said, "I have a seven-year-old girl named Geraldine. Are you willing to accept her in your life?" There was a pronounced silence on the line. As the tears formed in my eyes, I caught Maggie's attention, and we decided that we should take a day to think about it and contact the Sister the next day. She agreed. The next morning, we awoke with fixed smiles on our faces. It was the first day of the rest of our lives.

I'm not sure how much you know about adoption, or how much you know about Haiti, but speaking from personal experience, both can be incredibly difficult. Combining the two is not for the faint of heart, and it was especially difficult after an earthquake that had shattered so many lives. Life had decided to take us in an unexpected direction that we were certainly not prepared for.

It took more than a year of paperwork (dealing with both U.S. and Haitian governments) before we got the call to fly to the island to meet our daughter. Our trip took a week, as we had to go to various courts, sign papers, present as a couple, and pass inspections. It happened to be the one-year anniversary of the earthquake, and much was being made of the milestone. While we were in Haiti we were invited to stay with the Missionaries of Charity Sisters, at their guesthouse. Their site became our living quarters—the grounds covered the Sisters' home, a chapel, a school, and a building that served as a home for sick and dying children.

Anyone who spends time in Haiti will be transformed. Upon landing, you are enveloped in deep heat, brilliant color, and remarkable sound. Driving through the town of Port au Prince is a unique experience—there are no words to describe the emotions that run through your body. I saw cement buildings that had been collapsed by the quake, miles of tight and tiny shacks, and people wandering everywhere. On the roadside, you can buy anything from Cheetos to motor oil from eager vendors who walk many miles into town, morning and evening, just to secure a small spot on the road. As for the infrastructure, the roads will shred any vehicle in short order. Medical care is all but non-existent. And this is just the city itself—the surrounding countryside is a story of its own.

Haiti is a place that draws you in and pierces your soul. A single visit will change everything you think you know. The residents are poorer than we can imagine, yet they live their identity in the way they dress, in their willingness to work hard, and in their emphasis on family. There is a sense of joy, and if you listen closely, you may hear the singing of old hymns (in Creole, of course).

While there, you learn to appreciate what you have, and you may be overcome by sadness at the islanders' struggles. But more important, you notice their simple and humble contentment—something I believe we thirst for in our own "first-world" society. These are people who take pride in who they are, rather than what they have. They understand that true wealth is emotional and spiritual. I'm reminded of one of the New Testament Beatitudes—"Blessed are the poor in spirit, for theirs is the kingdom of heaven." I never understood that before I went to Haiti, but I do now.

So we received the awesome gift of a week with our beautiful daughter. During the trip, we spent most of our time onsite with the Sisters. We played with the children and helped where we could. Most of the children were going to be adopted by other families in the Twin Cities, and some of those families were down there with us at the time. So we had quite a network of people to help with paperwork, moral support, etc. These children would all be going to a place where they can continue their lives together. At that point, we still had a long way to go before we would be able to bring her home, but this filled our buckets, which had been getting quite empty.

This book is also inspired by another part of this story. Mother Teresa founded the Sisters of Missionaries of Charity in Calcutta. These women have dedicated their lives to the "least among us," and serve them with all of their being. Think of the places in the world you would never want to go, consider the destitute and the sick—those banished, forgotten, and avoided by society. This is where these Sisters set up shop, if only to hold the hand of a person in his or her last earthly moments, so they don't have to be alone. They are nothing short of an army; volunteers who have chosen to give up everything that we in the West hold dear and measure our lives by. They leave their biological families, abandon all material things, and devote their lives to service. Watching them work, spending time with them, and attending mass with them are experiences I will always carry with me. I remember going back to my room some afternoons, overcome with tears and grief. I wasn't sure at the time if it was the sheer poverty, the joy of finally meeting my daughter, or the work that these women were doing. Today, however, I am convinced it was the latter.

Haiti helped me see the world in a different light. Being put into a situation so different from what I was used to showed me that I had put certain "priorities" on my own back burner.

While I am fully aware that I'm not the first person to travel to a third-world country to come home reformed and wanting to make a difference, I believe I discovered something very interesting: I recognized that the same things that were unsettling me about my client relationships were happening in my own life.

There are conversations we need to have with our families, our communities, and ourselves and there isn't a minute to spare. As you read this book, the direct nature of the topics it covers may cause you to feel a bit overwhelmed, or even gloomy. Hang in there and trudge on, as we are simply peeling back layers that have been there a long time. Sunshine awaits you.

I fully understand that celebrating the blessings of this world makes for a great outlook, and a fulfilling life. But there are some things we need to work through. This reading is not a list of things you need to do, but hopefully an experience that will open a powerful eye and enable you to draw your own conclusions and apply them in your own life. At the end of each chapter, you'll find a few challenges for consideration. These are intended to help you progress from reading to reflection, and then hopefully to action.

Let's go change the world.

By the way, we were finally joined with Geraldine on June 25th, 2012. Since then, we have also adopted a son, Evan, who came to us on April 1st, 2014. They grew up together in Haiti, and will now continue their lives together. Geraldine Colin Stoerzinger and Evenson Barthelemy Stoerzinger are two miraculous works of art, and I am so grateful for them. They've changed my heart—and my life.

Mesi Jezi
(That's Creole for "Thank you, Jesus.")

Chapter One

∞∞∞∞∞∞∞∞∞∞∞∞∞∞∞∞∞

Money, It's Time for You to Know

MONEY. Just sit and look at that word for a while.

Money has been around since the beginning of time. For thousands of years, and in many forms, it has been used as an agreed-upon medium of exchange. One person works to gather up money until they have enough to purchase things they need. The person they purchase those items from accepts that the amount is satisfactory for the goods they are selling. This is the basic framework that most societies have been built upon throughout history. Of course, there have always been those who have more and those who have less. Some build empires for themselves, and others are unable to secure even small amounts. Money has been used for good, and for purposes that are not so good. Let's start by taking a snapshot of money in our current world:

Portfolio management. Behavioral finance. Status. Debt consolidation. Car lease. Wealth. Student loan. **Anxiety.** *Estate planning. Withdrawal fees. Penny stocks.* **Insomnia.** *Insurance premiums. Membership fees. Power. Late charges. Mortgage rates. Taxes. Globalization. Poverty.* **Gratitude.** *Bull market. Bear market. Black Friday. Margin. Inflation. Minimum wage.* **Entitlement.** *Wall Street. Retirement.* **Happiness.** *Inheritance. Capital gains.* **Safety.** *Extreme Success. Two-parent working family. Budget. Over-extension.* **Depression.** *High blood pressure. Commission.* **Significance.** *Property tax. Clearance sale. Investment selection. Get rich quick. Part time.* **Freedom.** *Overtime. Garage sale. Unemployment.* **Opportunity.** *Pyramid scheme. Golden parachute. Housing bubble. Competition. Ignorance.* **Fear.** *Birth. Life. Death. Income gap, rainy-day funds, and Christmas presents.*

The way we look at money today is extremely complex. It is the center of our culture, and something everyone needs to live. While many in this country consider money a basic means of existence, it has become so much more than that in many ways, even for them. Money determines where you live, whom you spend your time with, where your children go to school, what you eat, how you spend your leisure time, and so on. Most of us become comfortable making a certain level of income, and then the rest of our lives start to fit, piece by piece, into the opportunities that are available to that level of society. Fair enough. But let me ask you a question: What does money truly mean to you?

For more than two decades, I have spent my days talking to people about money. I have worked with people from all walks of life, with different incomes and wealth levels, and different attitudes about money. Some people start with nothing and work their way to the top; others have very little and inherit millions. Some spend their money the same way their parents did because they grew up on the farm and every penny counted. Yet others with the same background do exactly the opposite because, having been raised poor, they feel they deserve to spend their money. I've watched people save all their wealth until the end, and then spend it on health care. I've seen family fights you wouldn't imagine, and generational businesses thrive due to proper planning. I've been to weddings that have been saved for, and been a pallbearer at clients' funerals.

It's a wonderful way to make a living; simply talking to people about what is most important to them. It's emotional. It's important. It's life.

We are bombarded with information that ultimately relates to money. Do you need a new car? How is your portfolio doing right now, and should you be doing something about it? Are your children all they should be compared to the other children in the community? Is carrying a large load of debt okay? Is it normal to spend three hours per day commuting to and from work? Wouldn't it be nice to volunteer more? What are you going to do with your money when you die?

We are so overwhelmed by the forces coming at us that it is extremely difficult to step back and notice just how fast-paced things have become. Is this merely the 21st century version of "life in America?" Is it "all good?" Compared to most of the world, throughout history, we are off the map when it comes to success and human luxury. However, if I could make a presumptuous observation, many of us are running full speed ahead and becoming wildly successful, but we don't have a sense of we're headed. I contend that the primary reason for this is something I call the values gap: **The disparity between what we say is most important to us and how we actually live our lives.** Not how we feel, but what we do. We spend much of our time these days sorting through information, seeking to understand, but it seems we are having a heck of a time understanding what it is we seek. This is the question I wish to explore with you by sharing observation and insight. Let's talk about it.

Why would I lay out a possibly controversial scenario—in chapter one no less—talking about money and values, two things that we most often keep to ourselves? After all, aren't values something that each person has a right to have for themselves? Isn't it your business what you do with your money? Those are both true statements. But what's worse—struggling to find meaning in our lives, or not talking about it? I have dedicated my life to studying economics, money management, and behavioral finance. I have seen many wonderful people struggle with what they know to be true in their hearts and with the often-clashing demands of our world as they merge with finances. This gap is affecting our lives, and we can't close it if we don't discuss it.

Proof Positive

One doesn't have to look far to understand that money can bring varying emotions and levels of complication to our world. Think back to how money was for you growing up. How has that made you who you are today? What is your level of global investment knowledge? How much do you understand about cash flow, no matter how much money you make?

We all come from different backgrounds, and we have varying education levels and life interests. Yet, we all have to live in the same world. That's a good thing. However, I contend that we have moved from a *need* society to a *want* society in a fairly short period of time. This has affected all of us, from top to bottom. Think back to that American psychologist Abraham Maslow and his "Hierarchy of Needs." Maslow puts the most basic human needs at the bottom of the pyramid, and the less basic, more psychological "wants" at the top.

But sprinkle some prebuilt "want" into an entire culture and it seems like the hierarchy gets a little mixed up. This simple step has driven a wedge between us and what we say we value. I wonder what Mr. Maslow would say about all of this. Here are just a few of the symptoms.

Work/Life

Take a peek into the lives of the typical American family and you will see people who are busy. There is soccer practice, late nights at work, lots of fast food, technology, travel, community image, and a whole host of what defines us as "people" these days. There is true value in hard work, and blessings in all we gain from it, but what in the world could possibly make us work that hard?

Investment behavior

Aren't you glad that you have access to information about the markets twenty-four hours a day, seven days a week? We can turn on the television or computer at any time and see what someone thinks we should do RIGHT NOW. It's amazing, considering they have never even met us. The entire structure of how we think about long-term savings has changed over the past generation. We now look at our portfolios daily, and attempt to predict how this information will affect our lives in thirty years. We give cookies baking in the oven more consideration than we do our wealth management plans. The amount of money-related stress the typical American investor takes on—and the behavior it encourages—is mind numbing. This has to stop.

Just-in-Time Lifestyle

Have you ever spoken to a friend or family member who told you they recently went to their local "Big Box" store and paid five dollars for a pair of jeans? Yet, somehow in the same conversation, they want to complain about jobs moving overseas, evil corporations, or the government? I'll let you in on a little secret. There are many significant changes in the new economy that have made it possible for you to pay five dollars for a pair of jeans. However, the things we complain about are often times the dual side of which we perceive to be benefits. We need to acquire a long-term understanding of what we value as it relates to our lifestyles.

Life in a box

We tend to decide how much money we would like to make and then seek out a job that will pay it. This leads to unbalanced commitment and often unhappiness, which affects all other parts of our lives. I wonder what kind of world this would be if things were reversed, and we all lived out our passions and then watched the money follow.

Service Above self

Have you ever thought about becoming more involved in your community? The one thing that I believe makes America a light in the world is our history of serving our fellow man. This is changing before our very eyes, and I am deeply concerned about the long-term implications. Have you seen the average age of the ladies who do funeral luncheons? When is the next generation of helpers coming?

America, the Debt Machine

In the decade following World War II, America experienced one of the best economic growth periods in history. This brought the dawn of consumerism, and changes in eating patterns, transportation, housing, and general lifestyle—the white picket fence. The television show *Leave It to Beaver* was meant to showcase for all things idyllically American at the time: family stability, healthy interaction, humor, cozy furniture, shiny appliances, packed lunches, and interesting neighbors. The show demonstrated high standards and strong morals, with a household unit that communicated appropriately, dined together, and experienced all of suburban life's activities—with fun music to roll the credits. And while the

American Dream was a high benchmark, it gave viewers a sense of shared morals and national traditions. We all wanted a strong mother and father, a clean yard, and a family automobile. It was good living.

Moving forward into the 1960s and 70s, women's and civil rights movements shifted our cultural structure and led to a more vigorous workforce. Dad was no longer the sole breadwinner, and job conventions changed completely. Working to make a better life and climb the economic/social ladder became a way of life for many people, rather than merely a dream. However, climbing the ladder took priority over family time and conservative customs. Here we saw the introduction of community competition—"keeping up with the Joneses." There was a shift from mere survival to privilege, and we liked it! This felt powerful, dynamic, and right in line with basic capitalism. For the first time, we thought that buying things would make us feel better. We told ourselves that we deserved good things, and we happily made compromises to get them.

This era established a solid American middle class. We built a version of the Dream that meant owning a home. Government-funded GI loans allowed families to purchase property and take on debt to meet the demands of this dream. Every one of these new homes, of course, required a garage and a car. Few families had the money to buy a car, let alone the television and refrigerator they needed to make life complete. This was when borrowing was born; in a frighteningly short period of time, the American consumer was given two new members of the family: the house payment and the auto payment. Debt was introduced as an answer to everyday problems.

The next phase of history brought mass credit. In our race to succeed, we decided that borrowing money was a good thing. Initially, we started with higher-ticket items—homes, cars, and appliances—but soon we expanded our buying obsessions into all sorts of things: clothing, vacations, toasters, restaurant dinners, toys, and concert tickets. Newest to the game is educational debt, which is now finally showing its head as an economic reality for people of all ages. For many, the search for a decent living and higher learning has become quicksand.

The Values Gap

Let me ask you a question: What do you value most in life? Your family? Your faith? Your health? How much time do you spend each day on the things you say you value most? In theory, we should all be trying to get as close to 100 percent as possible. Now we are getting to the heart of the matter. We are living in a world that has become unkind, and is often in direct conflict with the things that matter most.

What do I mean by this?

I mean that it's difficult to live a modest lifestyle these days, because everywhere we go, someone is saying that whatever we have isn't good enough. One of the biggest problems in marriage is money. I mean, we have let the government fool us into thinking that the hard-earned money we pay in taxes is not ours, but theirs, even though there is silent outrage at how they spend it. The two-parent, one-income family is disappearing off the map and we act like the reason why is a mystery. I mean there is more to this world than determining whether someone is rich or poor.

We all come to the table with a certain set of parameters that guide the ways we live our lives. We learned them from our parents, and their parents, and their parents' parents. There is a feeling all around us that something has changed. Yet, whether due to our own choices, lack of awareness, or just a feeling of being overwhelmed, we let the values gap grow.

In her article *Satisfaction and Values*, author and founder of Money Quotient, Carol Anderson says, "Values provide both the purpose for our activities and the criteria for how we allocate our personal resources of time, energy, skills, and money. When there is incongruence between our values and the way we 'spend' those resources, inner conflict or dissatisfaction will result."

It's easy to build a list of things we all think are wrong with this world. This is not my intention. However, if we are to understand how to align our lives with what we value, especially as it relates to money, we need to understand what we are up against.

What went through your mind the day you closed on the purchase of your new home? Was it just money, or were there some emotions involved? What if you lost your job tomorrow? How does it feel when you make a significant charitable donation? Are these things just the consequences of choices we make on the road of life? Are they merely things that happen to us? There is a lot more going on behind the scenes, even though it can feel a bit like life on autopilot.

Any decision—big or small—has moving parts. There is not and can never be a "perfect decision." We must aim for balance, keeping our values intact and our motivations healthy. We can understand the decision-making process as a synthesis of four categories, and whether we know it or not, all these areas affect our behavior. Making good choices means we pay attention to each kind of cause and intent.

On the surface, it appears that most of our brainpower looks to the **"financial"** aspect of things. This is the utilitarian view, so to speak. However, the **"emotional"** considerations appear, and these memories and feelings help determine how we feel about money. The **"intellectual"** part plays a role in the way we process and reason. This is logic at work. The **"spiritual"** area leads us to see the greater direction of our decisions, and give a sense of meaning. The interplay of all these things brings completeness and enables us to make sound (money) decisions.

See for yourself: The center is where your best choices will be made.

DECISIONS, DECISIONS!

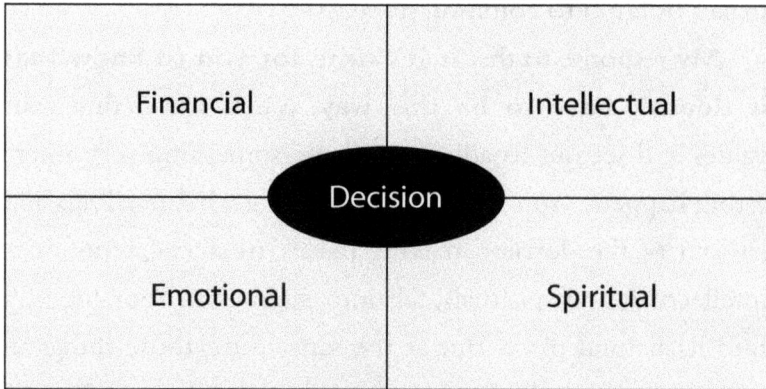

Financial	Intellectual
Emotional	Spiritual

Decision

Decisions can either promote our values or lead us away from them. When you think about it, defining your values should be one of the easiest things in the world. It's what you believe about God. It's how you want to raise your children. It's what you want to spend your free time doing. It's your cultural history. It is simply who you are. Not what I think about you, but what *you* think about you. That's it. And if it is "who we are," one would think that the most natural and enriching path would be to "be" who we are in all aspects of our lives. This means we can live like we own the clock twenty-four hours a day, because we do.

There are many reasons why we may have gotten a little off the rails in this country in terms of how we think about money. Some may say that it is just part of our natural progression. Others will say that consumerism has taken over, and the problem is now too large to overcome; maybe success makes us blind to common sense.

My response to that is, **it's time for you to know that it doesn't have to be this way**. When you define your values and set out to adhere to them, something very interesting happens: You move closer to living a balanced life, and all four of the decision-making pieces, (financial, emotional, intellectual, and spiritual), fall into alignment. Your life will find its natural place. But at the same time, those things in our world that seek to lure us away from our home base start to drift further and further away. They become less and less important. It's a pretty good deal.

Life in these United States of America is good. We have achieved success the likes of which the world has never seen. But now we question the lives we have built for ourselves, and the order in which we place the various pieces. We are now at the stage where it would do some good if the pendulum could swing back the other way a bit, and we could all settle into the greater understanding of how money works in our lives, and the simple graces it provides. We only get one chance in this world. One.

"MONEY"

There is at the center of all bad and good
A terrene possession. Let it be as it should.
We spend it and save it. Earning more each new day.
We tax it and lend … Even give it away.
The thing we call money. There isn't a guide.
Yet life and its meaning seem so intertwined.
Some people have plenty and some folks have none.
The reasons for this? Well, my friend, there are tons.
Nothing between us can tear us apart,
A dispute over money—It strikes through the heart.
Conversely, I tell you the good that is done,
In this world, from our tender is equal to none.
So how do we handle a two-sided knife
With the power to drown us yet give strength to our life?
It's the ultimate freedom. Just what should you do?
You should do what is right! But according to who?
Maybe our focus could be on its place.
Let it not be our God, but a tool we embrace.
You can harness its power and use it for good
When you honor its value and live as you should.

CONSIDERATIONS

1. Make a list of your most important values. Why are these things meaningful to you?

2. Identify a relationship that has been blocked due to money. What happened with communication? What's keeping you from reconnecting with that person now?

3. Think about what money was like for you while you were growing up. What did your parents teach you about money? What did they show you? How has that shaped the decisions you make today?

4. What is the best decision you ever made involving money?

TRIPLE DOG DARE

Try to live on 50 percent of what you normally make for one year.

Chapter Two

Before the Day After

ELMER and Eva have lived a fairly traditional American life for folks who were part of the WWII generation. They have been married for over sixty years. The couple lives in the same old blue house they built for $11,000 back in 1950, right before Elmer was sent to Korea. The timing wasn't perfect, since Eva had a two-year-old at home and another one on the way. But in the end, things worked out. Elmer came home, time passed, and life was grand.

Elmer had a good job at "the company," and worked his way up over the years. Eva stayed home to raise their two daughters. She was a loving mother, and known for her cooking. When it came to family business, Elmer pulled the strings. He managed the finances, paid the bills, and made the decisions. He always consulted Eva to make her feel a part of things, but she deferred to him in all matters relating to the "business stuff." She always joked that if anything should ever happen to Elmer, she wouldn't even know where to find the savings account booklet.

One Thursday morning Elmer was out working in the back yard. Eva called him in for some coffee, but he didn't answer. She went out to see what trouble he had gotten himself into, and there he was, lying on the ground. Dead.

It's the day after. Eva sits at the kitchen table, alone. Her mind races through the last sixty years of her life. It's quiet—too quiet. The grief is overwhelming, yet decisions must be made. Family members will be coming over soon. They want to go through pictures and belongings. Everyone wants to know if they can help. And then it hits her—how will she even keep a roof over her head?

When we grieve for someone close to us, the last thing we should be thinking about is finances. Yet, it is a part of life and we all must go through it. Even though there are strong cultural forces at work, especially for the "greatest generation," there are things that must be done to prepare financially for the loss of a loved one.

Elmer and Eva chose to take on certain roles, which probably worked well for most of their lives together. However, now—for the first time—Eva will have to tackle life insurance policies, bank and investment accounts, land and property ownership, health insurance, Social Security, Elmer's pension, and other legal paperwork. This can be truly devastating, especially at a time when life makes little sense, emotionally.

Elmer always took pride in the decision-making, but over the last few years, he'd let things slip a little. Paperwork was a headache; the terminology was always changing. So not only was Eva without access to information (by her own choice), but both of their daughters were in the dark as well. Even though they spent years asking Mom and Dad to sit down and go through everything, something always got in the way. Trying to help their mother now, amid all the chaos, who knows what they will find? Were things labeled correctly? Will they find the right files? Can Mom stay in the house? Will there be enough money?

So what do you think of this story? Have you ever experienced something like this in your own family? Are you going through it right now? Maybe you have something totally different but equally important going on, like the sudden death of a younger family member, pre-planning for long-term care, or dealing with a loss that happened some time ago. These are just examples of the kinds of things that come into play when we think about planning for living, and for dying. They are big topics, but after all, they are what life is truly all about.

Planning

Why is it hard for so many of us to plan for the day when we are no longer here? What would make us not prepare enough to leave things in the best possible state for those we love, even though this is often our greatest wish? The goal of this chapter is to address this issue, and to see if we can uncover some truths that will help us all learn what it means to plan "before the day after."

Think about where you are in your life right now. Live in the moment for a minute and give some deep thought to all the pieces of your life and how they connect. Think about your family, friends, material possessions, work, passions—all of it.

Now imagine that tomorrow you will be gone from this earth forever. What are the things that immediately come to mind? A simple fear of death? A feeling of things left to do? How will people cope without you? Would your family be financially able to survive without you? Are you prepared to go? Maybe you answered yes to the last question—maybe you always have your bags packed, so to speak. If this is the case, I want to say congratulations, because I believe this is one of the greatest accomplishments in all of life. Mark Twain once said, "Fear of death comes from a fear of life. A man who lives fully is prepared to die at any time."

Thinking about when we are going to die is uncomfortable for many of us. I get it. However, in order to get to the planning, I want to capture the feelings that planning evokes.

What makes a man not purchase enough life insurance to keep his family secure after he is gone? What causes parents not to plan properly for what would happen to their children if they both died accidentally? Why do we say things to each other when we part that we wouldn't want to stand as the last thing we ever said? How does a business owner not put a succession plan in place for his sons who have been working in the business for years? Are we too busy? Think of the time we put into things such as planning a vacation, or preparing for our sons and daughters to get married. Just think of the sheer amount of leisure time many of us have accumulated for ourselves.

We often have a mental block when it comes to making plans for the final act. How else could we tell ourselves things like, "I will get to it," or "it's too expensive"?

I am not a licensed psychologist (although sometimes I feel like one). However, I do want to offer some thoughts on how we think about matters such as legacy and estate planning. My first thought is this: Planning for the future doesn't mean you are going to die any sooner; It just means you don't have to worry about it anymore.

The emotional

Think about all the cultural fears we have about death and dying, and our "live for today" culture. Sometimes it just feels easier to put off planning our legacy, and our emotions have been fully trained to do this.

The worldly

Now think about all the material considerations that go into planning our personal legacies. Who will get the house, or the investments, or the lake property? How will the business ownership be split up fairly? How about the complexities of advanced planning, such as wills, trusts, and health care decisions—things most people don't have much experience in? What about our commitments to our communities and the charitable organizations we support? Managing our worldly blessings can be quite complicated.

I believe we must change not how we plan for our futures, but how we *think* about planning for our futures. We need to transfer our emotions from silo to multidimensional mode. Let's think about what we want to leave for our children based not only on what we think is best, but also on the mark they have left on us, and what they want us to leave them; not only the amount of money we leave to charity, but also what we leave to those who have helped us along the way; not the pile of things we have accumulated, but an inventory of the good we have done.

When we look at the future in this way, we transfer our emotions from fear to hope, because no matter what we say or do, we are spiritual beings, built to connect to those around us. We will place our worldly things into perspective, because our focus will shift from "what we own," to "the many ways in which we are blessed to share."

I believe this would represent an evolution in the way we think about legacy planning. It would help us make proactive decisions. These shifts in thinking, if they do occur, tend to show up at the very end of life. Let's move them to the present, for our benefit and the benefit of those we love.

Here are four key things to think about that relate to the subject of planning: First, be sure you have an accurate accounting of everything you own and owe, how it is titled, and how it transfers if something happens to you. Second, please take the time to enact whatever legal documents are needed to fulfill your wishes. Third, spend time really thinking about what you want your legacy to be. And fourth, please share your wishes and dreams with the people who are most important to you. All these things together make for a complete legacy, and missing any of them can have grave consequences. How often do we see someone not plan, and leave their family unprepared? Or they prepare financially, but they don't share their wishes with their family. You need all four wheels to make the car go.

For living ...

Johnny has been sick since he was nine months old. He is now seven, and has been through many surgeries. His mom is home with him full time. It has been stressful on the whole family, including his other two siblings.

It's an interesting thing about Johnny: While he is the one who has to suffer, he never seems to be affected by misfortune. For example, when the family is stuck in traffic and others are complaining, Johnny enjoys looking at all the cool cars. When there is "nothing to eat" in the house, he encourages everyone to sit down at the table together and have peanut butter sandwiches. And when rain disrupts the family's plans, he talks about the grass and how happy the farmers must be.

Some people look at Johnny and feel sorry for what he's been through. He's used to it. In fact, he is often confused by their concern for him. Actually, Johnny has been given special gifts. While he has endured trials few could handle, they contain hidden blessings. You see, this world and its distractions have never separated him from time. He lives in the moment because he doesn't know anything different.

Oh, there are tough days, physically. On those days Johnny retreats upstairs to his room, where his favorite saying hangs crookedly on the door, "When life becomes too much to stand … kneel."

Here's a twist on a question we asked previously: Imagine this—you wake up tomorrow morning and everything in your life has been taken from you. Your home, your job, your car, your bank accounts, everything! The rest of the world isn't gone; but *your* world has just changed. What thoughts are going through your mind? If all your material goods were suddenly stripped from you due to economic collapse, accident, or illness, what would you do? Where would you start? Now, ponder your life today, but in a different context. Are you living any differently than you would if you had nothing? Not from a necessity and leisure perspective, but an eternal one. Does it matter? Do you think about those sorts of things? You see, there will be a day when each and every one of us will lose all the things of this world. After all, that's going on right now, somewhere, for someone in this world. And every morning we are given the opportunity to practice for that day. The real question is not what *would* you do, but what *will* you do?

Have you ever noticed just how hard it is to live in the moment? We all know that we should stop and smell the roses, blah, blah, blah. We live in a world that makes it difficult to step back, relax, and just be. But there is a difference between living "for today" and living "in the moment." One places an emphasis on consumption and personal satisfaction; the other on reflection and being present. And it is by being fully present that we find joy in this world. It is wonderful when we take the time to do it, but somehow it is easy to fall away from. It's a funny thing. Kids seem to know how this world works. They are honest and curious with their questions— they don't hold back. They don't necessarily want answers; they simply want to talk, and mostly all they know is living in the present. They want to be with loved ones. Isn't that all any of us want?

Even after you've explained Grandpa's passing, your little girl will continue to ask about him for a very long time. To her, his presence is still real, and he's always a part of the family. She will maintain the spiritual side of his legacy. Children get it. People who have been in life-threatening circumstances often get it. Life's easy to take for granted … until it's too late. If you ask someone with a terminal illness what day it is, he will answer right away—it's likely the last August 3rd or November 22nd he will ever enjoy. Ask a random person in the elevator at work, and maybe, just maybe, she will know it's Thursday—but only because the next day is Friday.

As adults, we approach death (and oftentimes, life) with fear. Children have much to teach us, with their eyes to family, faith, and wonder. What a beautiful approach. We only have so much time on this planet, so let's get our priorities in order. At such a young age, it isn't fair that Johnny is sick. There are many people like him who know the value of life simply because they are more aware of it. Every day is precious to Johnny and his family. He certainly will leave a remarkable legacy, even if only to those closest to him. His lesson to us: Count your blessings and be prepared. Your legacy is not just what you want to be, but also what you already are.

If we are going to ponder the hereafter, we have to understand that we need to be thinking about the *here* just as much as the *after*. Remember, both the past and the future we discussed are shaped from the shadow we cast from the present, so it helps to step back and remind ourselves of that. It's easy to step outside and think that whatever is happening in the world is happening *to* us. But another approach is to dive into each day ready to "happen to the world." Either way, the results are tallied up and put in the record books for all time. Might as well show up for the game.

The bottom line is this: Like most things in life, having a clear picture of where you are today helps you plan for where you want to go tomorrow. I can't think of anywhere this is truer than in contemplating where you want to hang out for eternity.

... And for dying

Think about the last time you attended a funeral for someone very close to you. Picture the surroundings. Who else was there? What was the mood of the event? What was the family doing? Was it *your* family? What kind of day was it? Now think about the part when the pastor and family members reviewed the person's life. The room was filled with passion, tears, and memories.

You recall your own relationship with this person, and the feelings are overwhelming. There is joy for the privilege of having known them, sadness for what they leave behind, and respect for the many things they have accomplished. Suddenly the combination of feelings brings on a stream of new thoughts. You feel different. You want to celebrate life's gifts and take nothing for granted.

Maybe it has been days, or months, or years. Life goes on. Each person we encounter in life leaves a permanent imprint on us. Think back to that day—the day you walked away knowing you would never again take anything for granted. Today I encourage you to rekindle your thoughts for this person and celebrate them. They deserve it, and so do you. Let us never allow our memories of those we lose to fade away. May we always capture the blessings they brought to our lives, and live with the passion we felt in our hearts the day we said goodbye.

How many funerals have you been to in your life? Probably a bunch. Each of us will only die once, but we will experience death many times throughout our lives. We are all affected differently by it, and sometimes it seems easier to think about other people dying than to contemplate our own demise. The truth is, some people won't set foot in a funeral home even to mourn someone close to them, because they truly cannot handle it. Others cherish every minute of the opportunity because they know it is their last. Some people avoid it and think it will go away, and some suffer so much pain that they are never the same again. It is these reactions that I want to address.

Why are we so afraid to have conversations with ourselves about planning for our deaths and our legacies? Why is it so darn awkward? Let's see if I can hit any hot buttons. Maybe it's how you were raised—maybe your parents just didn't talk about death. Or you don't want to be reminded that you are getting older, or you don't want to make others feel that way. Maybe you don't want to talk to your parents right now because they might think you just want their money. Parents, the same goes for you regarding your kids. These are all very real fears. However, while we are all entitled to our own feelings, we are not entitled to our own facts.

What are the facts, you ask? The truth is that each and every one of us is going to die. There are many people in this world right now who haven't spoken to someone they love very much for years. But the things that separate us in life—pain and broken relationships and misunderstandings over money—are only temporary. At any given time, there is also hope.

Right now, there are people waiting to be healed by a simple phone call from a friend or family member. There are those in the world who have lost everything, and for whom a helping hand would change everything. There are those who are sick and alone, and being forced to contemplate their lives. There are those who are wondering what they have done, or what they can do. There are things to be forgiven, rekindled, shared, started, and finished. What do you have left to do? Look for them and I promise you, they will appear. They will be raw ... and powerful.

Here's an exercise to animate your thinking: Take a trip to a local cemetery. Park your car in the lot. Bring your coat, but leave your phone. Notice how the rhythm of your breath changes. Pace yourself, walking the grass-lined path, and notice everything with your senses. Feel the way time stops as the wind grazes your face. It's a peaceful place. Look at the headstones and see the differences in the dates. Some may be remarkably old. Are there crosses, angels, military markers, or other symbols? Is there a mausoleum? All these names! So many cultures, so many experiences! Every stone represents a human life. These were mothers, fathers, cousins, lovers, soldiers, accountants, and colleagues. They all had people counting on them. What kinds of legacies did they leave? Having walked among them, you are now a part of those stories. Think of your hopes and dreams as you sit on a bench in this cemetery. Who will lay flowers on your marker?

Your legacy is built by the choices you make. It goes on in time, and will be fixed into the hearts of loved ones by the stories they share about you. Goethe said, "Choose well; your choice is brief, and yet endless." We must plan carefully and follow through. Now is the time to think about the look and feel of your life—your purpose. Death is profound. The best thing that we can do is provide a sense of closure and peace for the people we take care of.

I know the role money plays in life and death. The logistical planning in your life is the keystone that will preserve the quality of life for you now, and for your family forever. You deserve a brilliant legacy. This is your chance to write an incredible story! Talk to your family about what you all mean to one another. Don't wait for bad news to take this seriously. Start today, asking specific questions and listening closely to the answers. Then get on with living. Let your life be a celebration, and share this joy with others.

If you do not know what you bring to this world, you will always believe its judgment of you—for if you truly knew, you would not have time to think about it because you would be too busy changing it.

" T R U E   W E A L T H "

What would you tell me if I asked you to say
What wealth means to you?
A request, if I may:
To talk about money is easy to do—
As the center of culture, it's what we pursue.
Our hearts may not mean it, but time after time,
It's how we are measured—the ladders we climb.
Life spent with others! More than one may contend,
"Nothing much matters, but family and friends."
They will always be with you, through the thick and the thin,
To support when you're losing and cheer when you win.
Maybe we're searching for more than this story.
A spiritual quest, bound by faith, hope, and glory?
They say the hereafter is what we're all for—
"You can't take it with you" is what they implore.
True Wealth, such a question, on the surface, so clear.
But it's more than a slogan of what we hold dear.
I think to define wealth, for life's truest sake:
It's what we can't buy … and death cannot take.

CONSIDERATIONS

1. Write an emotional will. Tie your emotional
   legacy to the actions you can take now.
   For example: I leave peace of mind to my kids
   and show them my love for learning, being a
   Dad who is home every night for help with
   homework; I leave security to my wife, having
   set all our finances into place and involving her
   in all family decisions; I leave my creativity to the
   world, having been a painter and a writer.

2. How have you gotten better over the years?
   How have age and maturity ripened you, made
   you wiser or more capable? What would you tell
   yourself at eighteen?

3. Who do you think is a good example of
   someone who is aging gracefully?

4. Write out a timeline of your life. Tape three
   sheets of paper together and start from birth,
   continuing to now with an extending arrow. Plot
   the things that have happened, see your decisions,
   and mark where you would like to be.

TRIPLE DOG DARE

Honor a deceased loved one by doing something he or she wanted to do but did not or could not do ("Someday I'm gonna ..."). Take a once-in-a-lifetime trip. Make the effort, take a risk, go out on a limb, and use their memory to improve the state of your own life.

Chapter Three

Talk to Your Parents

AS I write this, Thanksgiving is only a few days away. Millions of people across the country will drive to a family member's home to eat mashed potatoes and talk about how tall the children are growing. What a wonderful break, right? More and more, it appears our opinion of this holiday is changing—every year, the sales and sports games get louder and faster. What is Thanksgiving, at the heart? It means time with the people we're connected to, with a shared meal and certain traditions. Nowadays, spending intimate time together can feel uncomfortable, and often inconvenient.

On October 3, 1863, with the nation tangled in a bloody civil war, President Abraham Lincoln issued a proclamation making the last Thursday in November a national day of gratitude, creating the holiday we celebrate today. Lincoln's idea was that the holiday was to be a time of peace, rest, and sharing. Fast forward to today, when we're more interested in shopping. Lincoln knew that the family was the building block of our national identity, so he set aside time for us to gather in strength.

Some of us love Thanksgiving; others see it as woeful. Have you ever had the feeling, surrounded by relatives and turkey, that you really don't want to be there? Does it feel like too much work with too little personal space? This holiday meal is, after all, an exercise in the two things we struggle with most: food and family.

Thanksgiving Day is National Family History Day. How wonderful to have different generations at the table, sharing stories and relishing traditions together. It's an opportunity to see firsthand how a legacy works. Think about your own experiences, in childhood and as an adult. How has family togetherness and time at the table changed?

One of the greatest factors in all of our so-called problems is the breakdown of family structure. It's time to take a serious look at our priorities, and see whether we're following through on them. How well do we know the people we live with? And does it matter anymore?

Do we not spend time together because we're reluctant to do so? Or are we reluctant to do so because we don't spend time together?

When I was growing up in my own imperfect household, we were all together all the time. My uncles, aunts, and grandparents on my dad's side all lived within walking distance.

My mom's side was also very close by. I always had someone around to look after me, to right my wrongs, or to console me. Family brought structure and a sense of identity. I was a Stoerzinger long before I was an athlete, a student, or an American. It was a kind of "love you but don't always like you" atmosphere, as well as a backbone. I remember dinners and disagreements, and laughing and sharing. But most of all, I remember that we were always with each other. Family cohesion, as I see it, requires time, patience, generosity, honesty, traditions, and communication … but I have to admit, sometimes it's hard to put these into action. After all, we are people.

Remember when strong families used to be the norm? Now they're seen as kind of weird. Just watch any of the shows on television. What's that about? When did *wholesome* become a bad word?

What's the atmosphere at your own family Thanksgiving? What's your house like on a regular Tuesday evening? What do your kids have to teach you about the world? What can you learn from your parents? What can you give to your kids and your parents?

One Big Family

You may feel like a single point on your family line, but we have to understand how we are connected. Think of the generations before you, the hard work that had to be done in order for you to be here today. When we talk about our lives, we have to remember those we came from. Even the tiniest decision made by a great, great grandfather affects you. Our stories are theirs, and we are them. What do our decisions say about our families?

This is all driven by the term *legacy*. The way you live and the legacy you leave is all about the people you love. It's a family thing.

Throughout my life, it has been a wonderful experience meeting people from all walks of life. Old, young, blue collar, white collar—when I take a step back, I see patterns. Family dynamics tell everything, from what motivates a client to how they think about money (and what they do with their money). I ask to meet spouses and kids, not only to see interaction, but because these are the people I will be helping to protect. One of the most common patterns I see is the difficulty people have in talking to each other about money: Older folks fail to talk to their children about what will happen when they are gone, leaving those children to guess what their parents' wishes might have been. Dad owns a business and wants to transfer it to his children someday, yet he fails to put the appropriate planning in place to ensure smooth succession. A young man wants to go to college, but learns a week before graduation that his parents aren't going to give him any help. Parents don't discuss the nuts and bolts of money, so their kids don't understand that decisions have consequences, leaving them ill-prepared for life. Not talking about why we plan for things, aside from the actual investments. Making sure everyone's values are on the same page—if not in line, at least communicated.

You see what I am getting at here? At the center of financial planning, we have life planning.

Should we focus on making better decisions? Should we talk to the people we say we love? You'd better believe it.

Generation Gap

There are three parts of the equation to consider here: the kids, the parents, and the grandparents. All have importance in traditional society, with certain roles and purposes. We have unique ways of approaching the world. But how often do we avoid one another? Do we think that older people don't understand? Is it true that "kids today" don't care? There's a lot of love going to waste.

This chapter is about getting through those roadblocks. It's about being more compassionate toward one another and slowing down to reflect on the bigger picture.

You are not alone. That is a good thing!

In many ways, my late uncle shaped who I am today. We used to sit and talk for hours, about everything from politics to cars. Those memories will always be with me. To this day, one of my favorite things in the world is to go up to the lake and visit my grandfather. Just me and him. Time goes from a hundred miles an hour to zero, and I love it. After my two-hour nap, which usually takes place within ten minutes of my arrival, I am ready to go. My body tells me I am in a loving place. On the flip side, there is nothing more important to me than seeing my children process something for the first time, or the simple way they see things. It gives power to the thing that we call "family." We are all connected, from top to bottom.

Get to know your relatives, and I believe you'll feel better about the world around you. Thousands of years ago, we humans lived in little tribal units. We fed and protected one another from the natural world, kids and elders all living in collaboration. Thankfully, times have changed, but that doesn't mean we should lose our nature to nurture.

Discussions

We communicate with one another through storytelling. To every desire, dream, and fear, there is a story. Want to learn more about yourself? Want to know why you do the things you do? Listen to your family stories.

Find time with your mother. Drive out to your uncle's house. Have dinner with your dad. Meet them on their terms and be ready to learn. Everything you experience has already been done. Mom, where did you and Dad meet? What was the Depression like? What were your parents like? What did you do for fun? What was the worst job you ever had? What about a memorable vacation? When did you vote for the first time? What home remedies did you use? What food did you like as a kid? Did you have a garden? What was community service like?

Talk about family recipes. Talk about funny neighbors. Make the time, and you'll be richly rewarded. Let them reminisce. Magic will happen for everyone.

These kinds of questions will start other serious conversations. When priorities and values are out in the open, it's not so hard to ask about life insurance policies and wills. It's only conversation, anyway, not a firing squad.

Talk to your parents

Your parents are your reference point in this world. Like it or not, they are your teachers and guides. As children, we cling to them. Growing older, we form our own points of view, but something in us still longs for their approval. They've seen us in very vulnerable times. Depending on our age, we may be in awe of our parents, or we may feel embarrassed by them. But we should be grateful to them. It should be natural that we talk to our parents—about anything.

How well do you know your parents?

In the previous chapters, we talked about being prepared. Let's continue. How ready are your parents, legally, financially, and emotionally? Have you considered things from their point of view? Do you know their hopes and fears? When we talk about retirement or insurance, what we're really talking about is relationships ... and meaning. Look at the ways your parents are most vulnerable. Emotions are the base of every financial matter, so be ready to listen. No matter where you are in your relationship with them, listening is the most important tool.

Talk to your parents about money. Talk to them about purpose. Let your goal be to shine as much light on these matters as possible. Ask questions and propose solutions to problems. Don't assume the lawyer will get it all done. You can tell a lot about your parents by the way they spend their money. Moreover, it will help you better understand yourself.

Most parents will be honored by your interest. Let them know you are there to help; they dearly need (and want) someone on their side. Take one thing at a time:

- Do they have enough money to live on right now?

- Have they written a will?

- What would your parents like to do if they can't live on their own?

- Should they still be driving?

- How is their health?

- How are they meeting their expenses?

- Who pays the bills? Is that being done on time?

- How much medical intervention do they want in a worst-case scenario?

- Are they losing money they don't know about?

In the midst of sometimes stressful situations, this can be an astonishing bonding adventure. Even the deepest of wounds can mend when a family works together. Better still, you'll feel more confident in your own role as a parent. Let your children learn from your example—someday you will need them to help you in the same way. Teach them how to treat you!

You don't have any children? Then think about your own lasting effect on this world. Who are you, in the long line of history? What's your family's mark on the world?

Close to home

David and Susan are part of the "Baby Boomer" generation. Having done well for themselves, they were approaching retirement and looking forward to a new phase of life. As their careers were winding down, they had the flexibility to think about the transition. They wanted to spend time at the lake, volunteer, garden, and enjoy quality time together.

At the same time, Susan's eighty-six-year-old mother was wrestling with complicated health issues. Her father had passed away eleven years before. Susan was taking her mother to the doctor twice a week on average. One of four children, Susan was the primary caretaker; her brothers lived out of state and her sister had rigid work commitments. David, on the other hand, was an only child, and his parents were wonderfully healthy and self-sufficient. In her dealings with her mother's doctors, Susan began to understand that her mother needed increased care. Suddenly, Susan and David's retirement dreams were shifting, and things weren't going according to plan.

Does any of this sound familiar? Mom may have to leave the home she built with her husband fifty-two years ago. Naturally, she refuses to live in a nursing home. Susan is desperately trying to get a handle on her mom's finances. To her, selling the home seems the logical thing to do. But Susan soon realizes the mess her mother's finances are in—for one thing, she failed to update her will when her husband died. David steps in to help, but he feels caught in the middle of family shadows. At the same time, he's beginning to resent Susan's mother, whose neglect of her own finances is diminishing the retirement he and Susan worked so hard for. He wants to know why his wife's other siblings aren't available, and stress builds between all parties involved. Susan's mother feels shame and fear, David feels anger and frustration, Susan is defensive and exhausted, and the siblings only call to give their opinions about what Susan needs to do.

Mother feels like the fool of the family—helpless and overwhelmed. How can she expect to enjoy the end of her life, improve her health, and get through this financial panic on her own? She cries constantly. She feels like a terrible burden and suffers a loss of dignity.

Susan and David are forced to make decisions that have no best-case scenario. They've compromised their own finances and quality of life to put out dear Mother's fires. David has been sleeping on the couch most nights. There is no time for volunteer work, let alone daily activities. Everything now centers on the family catastrophe.

This scenario has become a very real and alarmingly fast-growing trend. The foundations of families fail when irresponsible or underprepared family members cannot pull their own weight. How will you, the "beneficiary," live and prosper if you are putting all your resources and energy into saving the sinking few? As overwhelming as it all may seem, there are ways to help the situation. Kids, sit down with your parents and talk. They need you.

Understand that your parents are well aware of the end of their lives. Please do your best to be flexible and patient and accept that they are out of their comfort zone. Be kind. They are doing the best they can.

If you are in a position like Susan's mother, please be as understanding as possible with your children. Consider their points of view, and recognize that they are trying to help. They don't want to talk about your money, your health, or your will any more than you do. They do not want to appear greedy, ungrateful, cold, or rude, but ignoring them will not make it all go away. Trust them. You've raised them, so trust that you've taught them well. Ask for help, and know that you are all in this together.

One thing I have learned about our culture's treatment of aging parents is that over time, the process becomes impersonal. Parents are taken farther and farther away from what is familiar to them. They have to make excruciating choices. No one wants to move out of their home, away from their neighbors. Your kids aren't trying to punish you. They are being pulled in many directions, and it is a strain for them to carve out time for caretaking. Daily life can turn into a list of tasks, and sometimes you may feel like an obligation. Certainly, emotional shutdown is tempting.

There's more

Talking is a good start—but it's really just the beginning. There are issues of peace, love, and forgiveness far beneath the inheritance funds. What to do with all these emotions?

As you get reacquainted with the people who brought you into this world, you'll find yourself feeling more alive and more accountable. Here are a few things to consider, things we need to say before it's too late. These are the sensitive topics we usually avoid, the kinds of things that influence our financial (and life) decisions:

1. **The Truth:** Let your parents know how you really feel (the good and the not so good). Your feelings will outlive your parents. Let them out now, while there is time to resolve them. Clear things up and be honest. It's good to do some spiritual housekeeping.

2. **Compassion:** Let them know you recognize the efforts they have made in this world. It's very powerful to be able to say to someone, "I understand." Everyone has sins, mistakes, failures, pain, and guilt. Though you were not around to observe, your parents endured broken hearts and tough circumstances, too. They did the best they could. Let them know you "get it." You may not approve of their actions, but you can certainly understand them.

3. **Gratitude:** Be thankful, out loud. These are, after all, the people who toilet-trained you. Thank

them for giving you life. Think of the good times and appreciate the opportunities they provided. Vacations, education, special outings, bicycles, time together, a room of your own—let them know how grateful you are for these things. I'm willing to bet there were times when you, the child, were neither loveable nor available. Their love is ultimately unconditional.

4. **Apologize and make amends.** We're all capable of being very mean. Whatever it is, take responsibility for your actions. A genuine "I'm sorry" allows two people to talk through a situation. This will be hard, but you won't regret it. Sometimes it's better to be kind than to be right.

5. **Forgiveness:** Resentment gets us nowhere. Forgiveness is humbling in any relationship, and it helps to say, "I love you so much and I am willing to set aside my pride in order to remain in your company." Let's move on to more important things. Forgiveness keeps us together, even when opinions clash. In the case of profound hurts, forgiveness can be a way to heal and move on. The pain may never be resolved, but at least we can gather our dignity.

Make the Effort

Love grows in our conversations. Let's know each other better, so we can treat what's ailing our society. When we make the effort to communicate, we heal. Even when the conversation doesn't go so smoothly, it can help us work through our emotions and past experiences.

Try, at least, to see where your mother is coming from. If you haven't spoken to your father in years, what's that all about? How can you gain a sense of peace about your parents, so that one day there is closure? What can you do today, on your end, to make every effort possible? We may not find the answers we are looking for, but at least we will know that we tried.

"Hello, Dad, it's been a while...."

Do you live with a parent-sized ache? Are you haunted by the lack of contact in your family relationships? I'm sorry.

In my own family, I've seen money and pride tear people apart, and it's heart-wrenching. But I also see optimistic light in my kids' eyes, and I can't let the past get in the way of their future. It's a conscious decision to move ahead. Your kids aren't just *from* you, they are *part of* you. Give them an open door, an open heart, and an open mind. What can we do? Grab hold of your remaining family, your spouse, kids, cousins, and neighbors, and squeeze every bit of the love you find there. Talk to them, take care of them, and be the one to set the structure. Get to know them and listen to them. The best possible legacy we can leave begins with forgiveness.

The Legacy

Most of us assume that the word *legacy* means the amount of money you have when you die and to whom it gets dispersed. I want to be known as a loving father, a supporter of my community, and a loyal husband. We want to know that we will matter, long after our time is through. In Ancient Egypt, legacies were immortalized with grand temples, pyramids, and hieroglyphics. But few of us leave tombs with jewels, so our true memory must be emotional. Above all, we desire to be remembered as good people.

Although a dollar can last for a while, consider the legacy of a conversation!

A legacy transcends time and assets. It includes both your accomplishments and your beliefs. It is an expression of optimism, compassion, and generosity. Ultimately, it is the footprint you leave behind.

Yes, you are a very important person. You have tremendous worth in this world. You may not know it or see it, but people love you—not because of what you have, but because of who you are.

It's in the stories we tell. What did we do with our time on Earth? How have things changed in your lifetime? How did you change in your lifetime? One day, you won't be in your usual chair on Thanksgiving. What stories will be told in your absence?

"Stuff" is in the legacy, too, to a certain extent. Homes, cars, bank accounts, silverware sets, and personal diaries will all be passed down and passed around; someone will get Uncle Joe's polka record collection. These kinds of things are proof of our existence. Of course, these are the tangible things other people fight over. In best-case scenarios, we create legal estates to provide for the ones we leave behind (this is where the lawyer comes in). Insurance, wills, and directives are invaluable for keeping security and peace. Therefore, the person leaving the legacy and writing the will should openly discuss his or her plans and wishes.

The legacy, in its truest form, is the way you improve life for the next generation. Friends, this is why we need to be talking to one another! It all comes down to our children. Do you read to your granddaughter when she comes over? That's your legacy. Have you started education funds for your own two kids? Are you a tutor, a Sunday school teacher, a coach, or a volunteer? That's your legacy.

Your legacy is what you give, minus what you take.

Memories

Have you ever had something happen to you that was so good that you had to tell someone about it as soon as possible? Maybe a new job, a first love, or an event with family or friends? Go back to one of those times right now. You can probably see, feel, hear, and smell everything as if it just happened. Ah, the power of memories!

When you finally got the chance to share your great story with someone, even your very best friend, have you ever felt that they were not as excited as you, or wished they just could have been there so they would understand?

Now think about the last time you were chosen to be part of someone's life-changing memory. Were you there with them living in the moment? Or was your mind somewhere else, maybe waiting to tell them something you thought was more important?

Imagine how different the world would be if we all made a conscious choice to live in the moment with those who mean much to us and their life events. Not only would we provide genuine affirmation to someone who thought enough of us to share, but we would also get to add these experiences to our own memories. Not a bad deal. Plus, next time, when it's our turn to share, we can be assured that someone is actually listening. No one is as important as we are!

By the way—Happy Thanksgiving. We have a lot of people to be grateful for.

THE BIRTHDAY WISH

It's Joe's tenth birthday today,
and he couldn't be more excited.
He has been waiting for months,
And every one of his friends and
family are coming over.
Joe lives in a modest part of town.
They don't have much,
but they get by.
Joe's father recently lost his job—
again—and his mother seems to
be very interested in the drink.
Joe and his twin sister
were hit by a car when they were
five years old.
Joe survived, but his sister did not.
The yard is filled with decorations,
and the cake is bigger
than he imagined it would be.
There have been rumors
of a new baseball glove.
Friends and family fill the small
blue house with food, fun, and
life—for now.
Joe has had quite a time
in his short life.
His health issues have been
limiting, physically and emotionally.
He misses his sister with
everything, and often wonders

why he is the one who lived.
The singing has stopped
and the candles are lit.
It is that special time
between everything going on,
when a young boy
makes his birthday wish.
Joe's mind is swimming. New gifts.
His hardships. His parents.
A better life.
His eyes were closed, but
he could feel everyone watching.
Just then, the good Lord
came to him and said,
"Joe, you have had your trials.
Please know this:
I am always with you,
and your sister is just fine.
I have chosen you for big things,
and will fill you with wisdom.
One day you will
see all things clearly."
Everyone was waiting
for the ten-year-old.
With a radiant expression,
Joe opened his eyes.
He looked around the room,
smiled, and simply said,
"My wish has already come true."

CONSIDERATIONS

1. Create a new family tradition, like a monthly game night, buying tickets to a baseball game in the summer, or an annual road trip to Grandma's house. You could have doughnuts on the morning of your kid's birthday, start a family book club, eat dinner on the patio in the summer, or visit a shelter once a month to feed the homeless—think outside the box.

2. Make a list of the things you are most grateful to your parents for.

3. Plan a family party in the summer. Invite everyone you can find, and spend a wonderful day together. Structure it so the old and the young are together. Ask the elders to tell their stories. Live in the moment, and make it a day for the children to remember forever.

TRIPLE DOG DARE

Think of that one person in your family who is really struggling. Maybe they have always struggled. Maybe you haven't spoken to them for years because of some bad choices they made. Maybe they personally hurt you and the reason things are the way they are today is 100 percent their fault. Go to them. Forgive them. Help them with what they need. Give without expecting anything in return. If it is too hard, then write them a letter. There is no harm in letting someone know they are not alone.

Chapter Four

Precious Time

HOW are things going in your life?

Does it feel as though you live on a rollercoaster? Would you like to finally quit the mindless ride of routine? What would it feel like to work only four days a week, with regular breaks and vacations? Does it seem like you are stuck? What if you threw out your phone, donated half your clothing, and changed your name from Robert to Bobby? How would it feel to see your family during daylight hours rather than trudging home after the kids have gone to bed? What if you quit worrying about not having enough money and acknowledged that you have plenty? Could you coach Little League instead of showing up late for the season playoffs? Take a walk with your spouse in the evening? Hold her hand?

You are one decision away from freedom.

It's easy to say, "I don't have the time." It's a tactic that we often use to protect ourselves. The question is, from what?

This is something many of us struggle with—but time is the ultimate equalizer. We all have the same 24 hours in a day to work things out, no matter our wealth, age, or occupation.

What are your priorities in life? What virtues drive those standards? Some people call them pillars, tenets, ideals, or goals. Own them.

Each and every one of these things is alive. Do you feed them? Do you hold to them? Do they drive your decisions?

When we say, "I don't have time," another way to look at it is to say that we've made a decision that other things are more important. Knowing our values and acting accordingly keeps us in touch with the right things and helps us prioritize. Otherwise, we can just go out every morning and do whatever the heck we want.

All the technology, the activities, the obligations—we are masters at maneuvering, yet we struggle in some of the easiest ways. We can manage high-level business operations and fly all over the globe; meanwhile, we lack time awareness in our personal lives. Today we have more resources than ever before. Our abilities, intelligence, and standard of living are grand. So why are we so lonely? How did we get so busy? How did we become so bored?

Is there joy in our lives? Is there desire? We all know how important it is to have relationships. Have we replaced our need for people with being busy? Are we missing the "free time" we are working so hard for?

What are we really doing with our schedules?

When will it all be "enough?"

The way we operate, by design, says that it's never enough. There are never enough minutes in the day, there is never enough cash, we never get enough attention, and there are too few days in the week. We're used to exhausting ourselves; hunger and frustration seem to be the acceptable norm. As for free time—we can barely afford it. When we do finally find a few minutes, there's no energy left. Searching for enough keeps us very busy!

It's your choice

Nothing happens by accident. Everything is a choice. I often wonder if we are volunteering ourselves to be unsatisfied. The busier we become, the more free time we long for. But when we gain free time, we tend to fill it with things that don't fill up our tanks. And so goes the pattern. Internet updates, shopping sprees, and television marathons? Cut them out. I dare you. Are the things you did today more important than the things you didn't do today?

Choose people. Always choose people.

"Yeah but ..."

Our families can be a deep source of inspiration. Do you feel that way? Is your family a support system or an obligation?

What are we afraid of? We're so harried that we barely have time to sit down for dinner together. Do we even want to? Yep! Let's have a little more discussion about being together and sharing a meal.

Most of us remember the good old days. Junior walks home from school with his best friend, a neighbor. Mom greets him while little sister plays in the den. A snack is prepared—something light to soothe Junior after an active day of recess and class. Mom brings in the mail, then packs up the children for quick errands—the bank and a trip to the market.

Back at home, Sister naps while Mom starts dinner. She chops vegetables, freshly selected from the produce displays, while Junior fills glasses with milk and sets the table. Father comes home at six o'clock sharp, to greet his son and kiss his wife on the cheek. The sun has set and dinner is on.

Father says grace, then turns to pass the rolls. "How was your math test, son?" he asks. There is a genuine dialogue, back and forth—discussion about Junior's upcoming field trip and Mother's plans for the front garden. They dig into spaghetti and meatballs, with sides of buttered green beans. After eating, the plates are taken to the kitchen sink (the children take turns performing this task, and the responsibility shifts from one to the other every week); a pint of whole dairy ice cream (vanilla with chocolate chips) is taken from the freezer and everyone gets a happy scoop. Then Father helps his son with his homework (with a careful eye to spelling) while Mom gives Sister a bath. Bedtime is consistent and firm, with a kiss on the cheek and a goodnight prayer. Father settles in the living room with a magazine while Mother has tea and writes a letter. Is this too old-fashioned for you?

Nostalgic, yes, but it really isn't a fantasy. There was a time, not too long ago, when traditional rituals were sacred. We had a stronger structure. When I was growing up, it seemed like everyone ate at home with the family. But today, things have changed significantly. As our kids grow older and activities increase, family time is decreasing. It's something all ages need—one of the most important things we can do for our families is eat together at the table.

The meal is the preparation, the passing of plates, the reminder to put napkins in laps, sharing the food, clearing, talking while dirty dishes soak (they can wait for a minute), and taking turns unloading the dishwasher. It is squash in the fall and asparagus in the springtime. It is excitement, boredom, and regularity. Conversation and food become integral parts of family communication; the formation of ritual.

Are you reading this and (like me) wondering what happened? The pace of life wasn't always so rushed. Eating together has incredible benefits: Families build stronger relationships, children do better in school and are better adjusted as teens and adults, and the entire family gets better nutrition.

Fast forward to now: Parents and kids don't communicate, and food has become a battleground. Home life has changed due to divorce, bankruptcy, and loneliness, and public health problems such as poor nutrition, diabetes, obesity, and eating disorders are rampant.

"You don't understand! I have a crazy schedule! It's impossible to get everyone together and hard enough even to zap something in the microwave!"

With a little thought and effort, we can easily find time to be with one another. Our priorities should dictate that family comes first. We can be flexible with our time, our activities, and our menus, but we cannot be flexible with our values.

What if we all silenced our phones and had a game night? Popped some popcorn and watched a movie? Can we stand one another enough to go camping? Visit a museum? Feed chocolate pudding to one another at the dinner table blindfolded? Or do you sigh and say you have to go to a meeting? It all sounds very wholesome. Wait. Isn't that what we are searching for?

Why do we work? To earn money and fulfill a need to be of service. To be able to pay for bills, housing needs, and weekend outings. We work to be able to live. If your wife were sick, you'd drop that meeting in a moment. Why not do it now, while she is well and vibrant? Make those memories. Are the guys in the office really that interesting to be with? Five years from now, you won't remember that meeting. You'll likely have moved on to another job altogether. But your family will always remember your love.

If life is made of choices, then the quality of our lives is also a choice.

Forward Motion

The way we use time has changed over the years. Two centuries ago, the schedule of American life was dictated by the rising and setting of the sun. We worked by seasons, sunlight, available resources, religious observations, marriages, births, weddings, and death. It was a natural cycle. Agriculture drove our markets, as did physical labor. Today, we have it easier than ever before. So how is it that we've become so out of tune with one another? We don't work together in the fields and stop for lunch, but does that mean it is okay to sit alone at our desks? We struggle to set boundaries. When does work end and personal time begin? Who comes first, the boss or the best friend? Are you the guy caught checking his e-mails on his phone at his daughter's wedding?

Life marches on, no matter where we are or what we are doing. The only moveable part in this equation is you and me: Time doesn't change—our use of it does.

Southern Europeans are famous for taking extended meals in the afternoon. Businesses close, people go home, colleagues meet in small cafés—it's irritating to us Americans on vacation, because we want to go and see and do. We aren't used to slowing down, and we certainly don't want to have our itineraries altered. In truth, I think we are a bit jealous. Let's remember that we are humans. We need balance. Right now, we're caught in the gap between how it used to be, how it's going to be, and how we wish it were. We can take care of ourselves and still be responsible workers. To use our time, we need to be willing to let go.

If Junior's story were revised in today's world, it would be very different. He would be dropped off from afterschool carpool, and he would let himself into an empty house. Since he hasn't eaten much, he's starving; the first thing he does is raid the refrigerator. He goes online and shoots bad guys until Mom comes home with drive-through sacks at seven (or eight-thirty, if she's working late for a deadline). She's brought Sister from daycare, and she is exhausted and has a massive headache. Junior eats his burger and fries while watching reality television. Mom tears through the day's mail (bills, card applications, and catalogues) without saying a word to either child.

Then Junior changes clothes and falls asleep on the couch with his iPhone. Dad is on another business trip.

Lather, rinse, repeat.

One of the biggest shifts in our families is the issue of technology. These are difficult boundaries to set. Suddenly, a live feed is more interesting than the people we are actually living with. How many times have you been to a party where everyone is looking down at their phones? Nowadays, two people on a date will both be texting. What are we even doing on the Internet? How much constructive relationship time are we missing? Sadly, we've quit telling our own stories. In the old days, we would take a question to a teacher or an elder. We'd look up information in the encyclopedia and start a discussion. Now we run to our computers. Where's the learning curve? Where's the lesson learned?

Technology can be a vampire. For all the wonders of modern communication, our expensive devices isolate us. Is a "like" a form of intimacy? Some restaurants have banned cell phones at the table during meals. Let's get back to being present—appreciating life's moments and not rushing away. What is your kid doing in the other room with that iPhone?

Meanwhile, the real world is waiting for you. Reality does not fit into a screen. How's the weather today? Go ahead, use the forecast app. Or you could glance out the window, or maybe even step outside to see for yourself.

The Pace of Life

What happened to the "good old days" when using time wisely was a way to nourish our lives? What's the point of working to provide for your family if you can't be there to share it?

My wife and I were recently invited to a get-together. We arrived at the time stated on the invitation, only to watch attendees trickle in. After a drink and an appetizer, everyone worked their way out. "Got to run!" was the apology—places to go, people to see. I've noticed this happening at a lot of parties and other gatherings in the past few years. No one wants to stay. We make an appearance and hit the road. If we don't have an imminent reason to go, we find one. I admit that I've done this myself.

Remember when you used to go to weddings, and the same number of people would be there at midnight, dancing and sweaty, cigarettes and all, as had been there at the start of the day? These days, it seems the productions are bigger, but the crowds cut out early. We seem to have a social itch that pushes on a very tight agenda.

I recall hearing stories about my father's parents back when he and his siblings were growing up. They would have parties on Saturday night that would last into the early morning hours. Then, the next day, everyone would come over to clean up and keep the party going. Everyone was invited: neighbors, friends, and family. There was food, drink, and most important, people sharing life.

Could you imagine having parties at your home these days, until very late at night, all the time? I can imagine all of the things you are probably thinking: *What about the kids? Work? We have so many other things to do. Hmmm.*

Another perspective

Joe has been retired for three years now. He is bored silly. Time is an excruciating topic for him, as he tries very hard to keep going. He is lonely, no matter how many people he sees every day. It's painful to think that his best years are behind him. Sure, he has plenty of money, and there are all kinds of trips and classes he could take, but he doesn't know what to do without deadlines, chaos, or a workspace. His wife is very involved with crafts, volunteering, and family, but he feels completely left behind. What's he supposed to do with his time? Wait until something happens?

Joe could use help. Having worked so hard for so many years, he feels he did everything right. But work was all he knew. It was his identity, and he overinvested in ways that don't pay back. Having missed so many parties, graduations, and recitals, he has little in common with the people he loves most.

The good news is that Joe has a wonderful wife. He will do anything to make her happy, so now he's accepting her invitation to "live." They are making plans to do things together, since she knows he is depressed on his own. More and more, he gets away from the television and spends time with her during the day. They have fallen in love all over again; he feels energized to take care of her in the ways he previously overlooked.

Joe's story has two morals: *Choose people*, and even better, *It's never too late*.

I urge you not to attach a monetary value to time. Follow your passion, and spend time doing what you really love. Relax. Your business will not fail. No one will call you lazy—they will probably be impressed! They may even be more mindful in their own lives. Any discomfort you feel, at least in the beginning, means you are heading in the right direction. Your value-based choices will open doors in new directions. Once you get a taste of freedom, you'll see that the possibilities are endless. You aren't cornered any longer, and you don't have to push. You'll be amazed, and your family will thank you.

Have a nice meal with a friend. Leave your phone in the other room. This is real life—don't miss it. Go ahead, have dessert—but share it.

Your life is waiting. Just imagine the prospects!

ICE CREAM

Remember when you were young,
And how much of a treat it was to have ice cream?
On a hot summer night,
you, your family, and maybe even the whole neighborhood
Would get out that old wooden churn
and make a wonderful concoction.
It was simply vanilla, because that's all there was.
Sitting on the front steps with your best friends,
Savoring every spoonful was nothing short of heaven.
Just thinking about it brings so many memories.
Now think about the last time you had ice cream.
Was it while you were driving?
Were you even with anyone?
Were you able to eat it all
Without thinking about how many calories you were consuming?
Do yourself a favor.
Go home tonight and gather a few of your neighbors.
Sit on the front steps for a long time
and share in some great conversation
While you enjoy a wonderful serving of your favorite ice cream.
You can go for a walk later.
You should worry never.
After all, what good is walking and worrying
if we can't take the time to celebrate
The little moments, which, strung together, make for a great life?

(If you haven't noticed, this story isn't really about ice cream…)

<u>CONSIDERATIONS</u>

1. Connect with nature. Commit to an interest and do it regularly. Meet with a club, go birding, take canyon hikes with your dog, go shelling at the beach, go kayaking on the lake, paint outdoors, see the bigger picture, and look at the sky. This world is full of wonders to de-stress and bless us.

2. Go to the library. Walk around, remembering what a library smells like. Touch the books and look things up. Check out some childhood favorites and read them at home, in your pajamas.

3. Eat dinner at home every night for three months. Take turns preparing, cooking, and serving. AND QUIT EATING IN YOUR CAR!

TRIPLE DOG DARE

Each day for the rest of your life, discover one
new thing. It could be a new book, a road
never taken, or something interesting someone
did. If you are alone, savor it and write it
in a journal. If you have someone to share
these experiences with, do them together and
discuss them at the end of each day.

Chapter Five

"Dude, Let's Buy a Castle!"

WHAT is your deepest, most awesome dream?

What are the excuses that keep you from it?

Why don't we live our dreams?

As children, we're told to follow our hearts, to listen to the voice within; we are encouraged to believe that we can reach for the stars. As adults, we replace all that with deadlines, taxes, expectations, finances, and fear. The transition keeps us feeling torn, believing we don't deserve it or can't possibly make it. Above all, we strive to fit in the safety of a box, confined by perimeters.

Thus far, we've talked about values and priorities. Now it's time to move on to dreams and imagination. These are priorities, too, and with our values in line, we can make these dreams come true. When wrapped in fear, we cannot be flexible. If a goal feels too luxurious or too good, we say we can't afford it. If it means that we'd have to sacrifice the comfort of control, we claim it's too expensive. Most of all, we don't want to step out of line. We don't want people to roll their eyes when we tell them of our great plan to visit Machu Picchu. Better to stay in the city and angle for the corner office. To follow your dreams would be irresponsible, right?

I don't think so.

How can we grow if we don't stretch our limits? And whatever happened to fun?

Financial worries are a great way to ruin fun. We don't have fun because paying off the mortgage is serious business. Maybe there's a business you want to start, but you hesitate because there are simply too many unknowns. What's happened to our entrepreneurial spirit?

We can be anyone we choose. It's a matter of easing off the worries and creating a plan of action. It means we surrender to the unknown, plan for the best, and prepare for the worst. And consider that you can do all of this (*carpe diem!*) and be completely responsible, too. I'm not saying we should abandon our families and quit our jobs to sail around the world on a yacht; I'm just trying to get back to the wonder of life that got us interested in the first place.

We all want to live better lives, so why do we accept "good enough?" And what happens when "good enough" isn't good anymore?

You and I can do anything we want, as long as we work

hard, have a vision, and bring others along with us on the journey.

With balanced principles and priorities, we can determine solid and healthy ways to budget and plan. We can live simply today, knowing the joy of participating fully in our own human lives.

Easier said than done, you might think. I used to feel the same way. I grew up like most people, setting college goals so that I could achieve business stability. I was prudent and careful in all my decisions and did things in the way that I was "supposed to." Then I met Peter Hill, who helped shake me from the norm and sparked a sense of curiosity in me. He taught me to ask more of life, to expect more. And he showed me how to create change.

So, it's a nice fall evening back in the early 2000s, and my phone rings. It's my very good friend Peter:

"Dude, plan on coming over to my house next Tuesday evening. We are going to buy a castle in France and I want to go over it with you."

I asked him if he was feeling okay, and without missing a beat, he began to explain the proposal in detail. It was very simple, he said. The two of us and some other folks were going to buy a castle in Soudon, France, and turn it into a bed and breakfast. Then he explained his fantastically complex financial and marketing plan.

So here's what we did: We bought a castle in France.

Here I am, today, like anyone else in the neighborhood. I wear a tie to work, shop for groceries, and hang out with the neighbors—and I can say that I've owned a castle in the French countryside. Sure, I put a fair amount of money into it, and it was a project we could not sustain, but it was one of my great adventures, and I proved, indeed, that anything is possible. I'm proud to have this story to tell.

I've heard it said that any story worth telling has a risk, and any story worth hearing has a dream. Peter taught me—showed me—that it's important to dream. I know that God put me here to enjoy life, not just to work and make money. We get to spend money, not just earn it, and our values and families can prosper from the decisions we make.

Unfortunately, I lost my dear friend to cancer on January 7th, 2011. Peter taught me the good side of fear, and to respect that strange electric sensation that settles in your belly when you're in an "impossible" situation. What if? Why not? He was a man who lived to live, and he was not the kind to ever say, "Someday, I'm going to …" He had an idea and made it happen.

With this friendship, I began to take my dreams more seriously. I believe that God puts things in our hearts for a very good reason.

Peter showed me how to live in color. And it was interesting to see such a bold personality in real life—he would wear an outlandish hat and pull it off with style, and make you think it might be something you'd want to try on yourself. He was an expert at developing relationships, and had a knack for finding his way into the most interesting opportunities. Whether doing artwork for a popular musician like Bon Jovi or deciding to buy a castle in France, failure was never an option. I wouldn't call him a dreamer so much as a man who was truly alive.

There are millions of Peters—and you and I can do the very same thing. Normal, regular people can have extraordinary lives, just as he did. Peter's essence wasn't about risk; it was about opportunity. Maybe you'd like to quit your necktie job and start a non-profit. That's a wonderful idea! But how will you live in the meantime? Try one step at a time. Start by diving into some volunteer work. Take time out of the office to show up more at home.

Making wise daily decisions allows us to be flexible when opportunity calls. Notice also that Peter had a plan of action with the castle idea, as with every one of his adventures. Most important, he took care of people along the way, and included them. His joy was shared, never singular. And he did things with a tremendous faith, confidence, and integrity that was rare and contagious. He made me want to be a better person, flaws and all.

In finance, we talk about the role of a budget. I believe we need a sort of life budget—how we spend and manage time, energy, activity, goals, and priorities. Time is precious, and we need to notice the ways in which we're spending it.

Why do we spend years nursing an unrealized dream, only to grow tired and disenchanted? Sure, we have struggles, but can't we live well in the meantime? I believe it's perfectly realistic to have incredible dreams.

Adopting my children was my own impossible dream. My wife and I charged into unknown and uncomfortable territory when we signed up to make ourselves a family. Me, a father? Responsible for the health and well-being of children? Me, traveling to a place where there are almost no rules, to hang out with Mother Teresa's Sisters? This wasn't the kind of thing I was set up to do. But the idea struck a beautiful chord, spiritually and emotionally, and the danger of it made perfect sense to my wife and me. We did what we felt was right and followed our hearts. And you'd better believe we had naysayers and second thoughts.

Meanwhile, I own and run my own business. I make a good living, but that's not the fun of it—it's the people I've come to know and love that I am so thankful for. I seek to provide a sense of security and build meaningful, lasting relationships. While most people might think a financial advisor is a pretty conventional role, I seek to prove them wrong. It's exciting to have professional success that allows me to be such an active and available member of my community. This is what I want to do, and it's what I love to do. It allows me to set and exceed goals that benefit clients, friends, family, and co-workers, while challenging myself to learn and mature.

Imagine if you didn't have the "big brother" forces telling you, "You need to make this much, you need to join this group, your kids must eat this cereal, you have to work at this desk, be here at this time, with a wife who is just this size …" Imagine what it would be like if it were just you, and you realized the ability to take full advantage of everything you are, of the gifts you have been given. Would your view be different?

How would the day look if you could choose your sunrise and sunset? What if you didn't have to set an alarm in the morning? What can you enjoy now, before you retire? Before you realize how much time you have wasted worrying?

What are your intentions, and how do you need to refocus? What would it take for you to slow down (or speed up, if that's the case)? Can you find some time to rest, enroll in a class, pick up a hobby, or make a short trip to get you away from the "to do" lists? Once in a while, you run into someone who just seems to be lucky. They always seem to be doing whatever they want. Here's the truth: They probably aren't lucky. It's possible, my friend, and very important, to listen to your heart's desires. What if you watched a black-and-white show on television every night, and one day, you had it all in Technicolor?

When Peter passed away, I was unable to attend the funeral because I had to leave for Haiti the very same day. It was, I believe, the greatest honor I could've given my friend. Every decision he made seemed to be in line with his values and beliefs.

This is from the letter I wrote to be shared at Peter's funeral:

"You helped me realize that I should not only look forward to the future, but look forward to the present. That blazing a trail is better than following along. And helping people succeed, without expecting anything in return, is greater than any treasure you could gain on your own. For that, and many other things, I am ever grateful.

"One more thing:

"You spent much of your business life in the world of marketing, helping other people tell the world who they are. So I thought it would be appropriate if I could think of one final 'tagline' that would sum you up, Peter Hill. It didn't take me long.

"Live Life to the Fullest, and Ask Questions Later."

What holds us back from Technicolor? "Conforming ourselves to this world," so the Bible says. Not respecting our own boundaries, giving in to the demands of others, failing to stick to our priorities, putting things off because we feel scared, fearing that something we do might raise an eyebrow, wondering what other people will think, not embracing change, the need for routine, weak relationships, lack of confidence, ambivalence, taking too much care of other people, money, and well, not knowing your own dreams! You need no permission to live the life you were born for, except your own.

"A Common Passion"

What do you wish you could become if you could get up tomorrow morning with a clean slate and a box of crayons containing every color imaginable? As you draw your picture, these colors will represent the many facets of you, and your life as you create it.

What colors are you going to use? Here's a little secret: Each day when we arise, life presents us with a blank page to make our own. It may seem difficult because we are not given an eraser, and we cannot control everything in our surroundings. What we do have is free will, and the ability to treat each new situation with an attitude we have chosen. Life may never present equal opportunity, but it will always give us equal time to make the best of every situation. I believe we all have a common passion, to simply use the unique skills we have been given in a way that will benefit the world. The hardest part is often uncovering those gifts, and convincing ourselves we are worthy.

So what colors are you going to use? You'd better get started. No one ever gets to ninety years old and says, "I wish I'd been more careful!"

Live life to the fullest and ask questions later!

BE ON YOUR SIDE

We spend much of our existence,
Putting limits on our abilities.
The older we get,
The more we avoid "living."
We are rarely sure
About the things we do well,
But we're positive,
About things we could never do.
Step outside yourself,
And take a good look at your life.
Turn your dreams into goals,
And make your goals a reality.
Appreciate all that life brings.
Good and bad.
Don't worry …
There will always be someone
In life to knock you down.
Just be sure it's not you.

CONSIDERATIONS

1. What did you want to do with your life when you were ten years old? What got in the way? What is one thing you could do today to honor that?

2. Write a letter to your future self, the person you'll be a year from now. Write another to yourself one year ago. Open them both at this time next year.

3. What's the greatest risk you've ever taken? What was the outcome? How did you learn, and what motivated you?

TRIPLE DOG DARE

What is the best book you have ever read? Contact the author and tell them how much it meant to you, and how it changed your life. Tell them why their work matters to you.

Chapter Six

Helping Yourself and Serving Humanity

Lessons Learned On a Mountain

IN August 2013, Maggie, Geraldine, and I spent some time in Haiti preparing to adopt our son, Evan. On this trip we spent quite a bit of time "vacationing," exploring the country and taking in the scenery. We covered the big city of Port au Prince, meeting wonderful people and enjoying the food, and traveled up through the mountains. Situated between the ocean and a sea, the Caribbean scenery is stunningly beautiful. However, this island happens to be one of the poorest countries in the world.

One afternoon we were having lunch in the mountains, where we met some artists. These villagers lived in tiny shacks nearly at cloud level, on the side of a winding road with no guardrail; their lives were carved into the side of the hill. Each person shows his or her craft and hopes you buy something. As we prepared to leave, a man who had been particularly persistent begged us to go back with him to his area. His wares were smaller pieces that we hadn't stopped to look through. We said we would return the next day, as we still had to run another errand. The man gently clutched Maggie's arm and spoke, his watery eyes looking into our faces: "But I have to eat today!" In that instant, my life changed forever. Suddenly, my personal worries vanished.

Right this minute, there are millions of people on Earth who dearly need food and medical help. Most of us can go an entire lifetime without experiencing these kinds of fears—we are very lucky. But when you find yourself inches away from this kind of poverty it stops you dead in your tracks.

He was a kind of man I had never met before—it took my breath away. He held his head with stunning strength and dignity. He'll never know the effect he had on me.

You may be wondering why a financial advisor like me insists on relating poverty to modern financial planning. Aren't we supposed to accumulate money? Isn't it good to be rich? My goal is to remind us all that it isn't about the money. The idea behind the money is security. My professional goal is to make a comprehensive plan with someone to make sure they don't run out of money. However, in my opinion, the amount of money a person has isn't as important as what he or she does with it. When we strip away the facts and figures, money is all very emotional. We can't really make progress until we understand those emotions. I have found that most people don't necessarily want to be rich—they just don't want to be poor. Isn't that what we all want? Security?

What good is money management (or accumulation, for that matter) if we lose touch with one another? What if I hadn't had that eye-to-eye meeting with the artist on the hill? True, holistic financial planning is about developing a long-term road map that helps us live well in the moment.

For the first few days of my visit I had been in shock, noticing everything the Haitians did not have that I thought they needed: Imagine if they could see the traffic lights in America, the shopping malls, the clean sidewalks, the elevators, the air-conditioned supermarkets! But then I saw that the Haitians were focused solely, with appreciation, on the things they *did* have. There's a giant gap here, and it took some serious spiritual searching for me to finally "get it."

As we were getting ready to go down the mountain (after purchasing some of the gentleman's wares), we had a renewed sense of purpose in the trip. He gave a face to the discomfort we had been trying to avoid. This wasn't something we could throw money at; Haiti became a real situation with beating hearts.

No matter where you are in the world, there is a fine line between helping yourself and serving humanity, but it can work well if done correctly, and the two go hand in hand. As

I look back on our trip, I am reminded of the timeless quote from Mother Teresa, "If you can't feed a hundred people, then feed just one."

We didn't have to save anyone. What I understood, in the theme of this story, is that simple things are often the most effective. The man didn't ask us anything more than to support his livelihood and talent. He wanted to be acknowledged. We bought from him, not as charity, but because it filled a single need. It felt good to give, and he was proud to sell things he had made. He helped me feel more human. The small amount of money I gave him made sure he ate that night. In truth, it was a joy to participate. We can do the very same thing here in our own communities. We find a detail, a face, a corner, and we meet it.

This is what it means to be human. When we give, we receive—and we grow.

Community service

All great work begins close to home.

For many generations in America, service in our communities was the backbone of society. In the earliest years of colonization, rebellion, and revolution, our country was a network of hardworking individuals who cooperated in order to survive. Relocating from Europe meant we had to forge profound friendships in order to meet our basic needs. We helped each other farm, defend our homes, nourish ourselves, trade, and mature, shaping the identity of a multi-cultured new country. Once we got settled, the habit of philanthropy became a way for those who were prosperous to assist those in need. Historically, Americans have been very good about encouraging a higher quality of life. Etymologically, *philanthropy* means "love of humanity." Philanthropy develops and enhances what it is to be human for both the benefactors and the beneficiaries.

There is a difference between philanthropy and charity, although both have important roles in our society. Charity seeks to alleviate pain (serving dinner at a homeless shelter, for example), while philanthropy works on the root of the problem (for example, low-cost housing, education, job reentry programs for the homeless). We have always been a nation of people helping people. This is what gives us energy, as thinkers, dreamers, and entrepreneurs. Each of us has the right to life, liberty, and the pursuit of happiness; we are people of great hope.

Things have changed in the last few decades, as we've grown more and more accustomed to a different way of life. Our priorities seem to have shifted a bit, and we have become less and less community-minded. I understand that there are many more things going on in the world, but isn't it better to work together? Aren't goals more feasible when we help one another out? It's hard to trust and enjoy this world if you are afraid of it. The surest way to fight fear and greed is to remember that life is a group effort.

In every era of American history (and in many other cultures, as well), our problems have been solved by working together. During the Great Depression, we saw massive financial struggles, but that proved to be one of the country's most important bonding experiences. Our nation learned to take the humble swallow and keep going. President Roosevelt started a giant series of public works projects, encouraged soup kitchens, and gave his famed fireside chats on the radio for families listening at home. We were pointed toward simpler things and hard work, helping ease the blow of economic devastation. It was a desperate time, but an incredible learning experience. The money was gone, but we still had one another, and the wellsprings of volunteerism—clubs, missions, aid groups, and charity groups—soared. As a nation, we were grateful.

In every time of national growth and strife, the theme remains the same: community.

Think of the reaction to 9/11; in the following weeks, we felt closer as a nation. We proudly flew flags on houses and business fronts, walked our kids to school, and slowed down to appreciate daily life. We supported veteran's groups, donated to non-profits, and started showing up for church on Sundays.

But then the Stock Market fell and we panicked again— back to work, back to the daily grind. We had bills to pay. We lost the feeling of camaraderie. Now we spend hours with our screens and nearly zero time in community service.

In recent years, many social and health service organizations have struggled to find enough volunteers. Instead of concentrating on the agency's purpose, they scramble to cover basic needs. Think of all the ways volunteers carry weight in our lives—who puts the books on shelves in libraries? Who staffs the information desk at the hospital? Who tutors after school, organizes music at church, and plans afterschool activities for our youth? Economic pressures, changes in lifestyle, and new kinds of family composition have meant there are fewer volunteers available from traditional sources. Meanwhile, we have grown to expect the government to fund recreational, medical, and social programs.

The most important parts of a service agency are the volunteers. They are its heart, soul, helping hand, and compassionate face. Fundamentally, it is people helping people, and this is where ministry begins.

When you need assistance, who will be there to help?

The Rotary Club, the Lions, the Boy Scouts, the local YMCA, PTA, church choir—these groups exist for a reason. People participate in them because their participation serves a purpose and makes them feel useful and less alone. How wonderful to take on projects, raise funds, discuss pressing issues, and open multicultural dialogue; to teach, to listen, and to learn. We give support to one another and have coffee afterward. We laugh, we cry, we make long-term goals, we see progress, and we raise our children together. Time goes by, and this is the stuff life is made from.

Giving should be a natural part of our schedules. *It is a part of our identity.*

There are many good reasons to volunteer. The formula for successful volunteering goes something like this: Provide opportunities for personal achievement, allow volunteers to make new discoveries about themselves and others, and let them appreciate the bonds they are forming to fortify their community. Mix with appropriate training, feedback, and recognition, and you have energized volunteers who feel better about others—and themselves. Our volunteer time adds a layer of richness to our lives.

With all that said, several factors have decreased our community involvement. Again, we are too busy. Often, we don't think we'll truly make a difference. Or it's the famous PTA meeting scenario: Sit in the back and hope that other people raise their hands to help. Some of us send money and feel it's enough.

There has been a shift away from civic involvement as we expect, more and more, that government will fill the gaps. It takes more than Congress to provide hope in this world. After all, they require volunteer work to get them elected! This is not a political statement—it's common sense. The purpose of government is to secure and organize our infrastructure and to defend against threats. It's up to you and me to work on the way we live.

Now is the time

If we want to change the world, let's get to it. Let's recognize that our back burner issues are very real and personal needs. The excuses that keep us from service are the same front burner things that keep us apart. If we quit giving, we miss the opportunity to show our children how to trust this world. What a great way to teach our kids to "Love thy neighbor."

When I refer to "giving," I mean participating in activities that require us to acknowledge the needs of other people. It builds a special kind of optimism that enables you to believe goodness is possible, no matter how hard or unfair the world is. Our current culture is taking this away. I've heard it said many times, "When you can't take it anymore, give."

Meeting people who need your help can be life changing.

So none of us have to try to change the entire world (although I'm certain you could). What I am asking is for you to reflect on your own world. Have you ever fed the homeless at a shelter? Coached a soccer team? Worked a blood drive? Doing these things may lead to a new job, new friendships, and less personal stress. You may find yourself entering the kind of life you've been wanting. If nothing else, it will help you feel more alive.

Get active and bring your family. Make it a tradition. Don't be afraid to put yourself out there—volunteering lets us take on new and interesting roles. Become an aide at a local museum. Chaperone school dances. Build shelters, volunteer to help on voting day, and walk dogs at the pound. Welcome home the troops! The more we bend, the less we will break.

Full circle

Recent research shows that people who volunteer live longer and have a better quality of life. If you are lonely, volunteering is one of the single best ways to form a social life and improve your emotional and physical health. The good feelings you experience when helping others may be just as important to your health as exercise and a healthy diet. When you see the product of your work (a grateful child, a new roof on a house, a man with a new pair of shoes), you'll know that you've made a tangible difference in the life of another person. That, my dear reader, is the greatest thing we can hope for.

No matter where you've been, no matter who you are—you are vital to the community. The funny thing is this: You may not know it just yet!

More than expected

Meals on Wheels is one of the best-known regular service organizations in America, a clear and simple example of real-life commitment. I have enjoyed being part of a Meals on Wheels rotation through my Rotary club for many years. It's a momentous way to step out of the daily routine. The basic premise is this: The volunteer delivers meals to a senior resident (or couple) in their area. You don't have to be a good cook, and it doesn't require a great amount of time, but you get to provide an elderly person with services that help them live a healthy and enjoyable life. The Meals on Wheels website says, "Perhaps as important as getting meals to seniors is your smiling face and some words of kindness and friendship. Many seniors are lonely, and those that assist in meal programs are their only daily contact with other people."

For me, it's been a fascinating experience. Admittedly, I'm like anyone else when it comes to volunteering. I often forget until the last minute, and I feel it is a hassle to interrupt my busy day with the dinner or lunch delivery. I have to leave work early, order and pick up, find the residence, get through traffic, and introduce myself to people I've never met before. My burning thought is, *Do I really have to do this?* But it's the same story every single time—as soon as I get to the front door, I'm glad I made the effort.

Meals on Wheels connects me with things I desperately need to witness. When the door opens, a face appears. Here we are, two human stories, meeting! My worries drop, and I feel gentler and saner. When I meet these people, I get to know a piece of living history. They've seen things I can hardly imagine. It humbles me to know that I may be their only contact with the "outer world" that day, or for many days. It's the least I can do to bring warm, delicious food to their home and provide a few moments of conversation. My short little appearance reminds them that they are not alone.

I leave the house feeling that I am not alone, either. My feeling when I leave is the same every time: Thankfulness. I'm so glad I made the effort. I got back more than I gave.

The feeling I get from volunteering is a spiritual high. It is healthier and lovelier than many things I might hope to achieve in this world. Knowing this, I encourage my family, friends, and co-workers to participate in this program. I want everyone I know to be in on this, to share in the growth and pleasure that comes from service.

In the end, it seems that we've let service become negotiable. We've replaced face time with Facebook. Let's not neglect this any longer. Service is a gift to be given, as well as received.

Let's replace what we've lost.

Even the Lord himself said the poor will always be with us. Of this I have no doubt, for he also said, "What you do for the least of my children, you also do to me."

One does not have to travel to the third world to save the poor. They are all around us. You think paying it forward is cool? Well, this is paying it forward for your soul.

I'm not just talking about buying Girl Scout cookies. (Although, feel free, as they are very good). Meet them where they are, look into their eyes, and let them know you care about their lives. You may be the only one who ever does.

So yes, there is more to life—there will always be more! There are things going on all over this world that make a person's eyes pop. There is agony and suffering the likes of which neither you nor I could ever imagine. You may be thinking, *Hey, Mr. Money Advisor, that's all well and good, but I am just trying to put food on the table for my own family. Nice of you to guilt trip me over the rest of civilization. It's hard enough as it is, right here in my head.* That, my friend, is one of the dangers of complacency. Notice the way we convince ourselves that "doing something" would be an onerous task, a chore, an obligation. My message to you is simple: Don't do less, do more. Seize the joy of service. We must do more. If we are lucky enough to be able to ask these kinds of questions, we have a responsibility to do something about it. And that is a good thing!

The Trip

After many years, Allison finally convinced Steve to go on a mission trip to Africa with some friends. She knew it would be good to get out of their comfort zones. He didn't want to go. He felt they had a good life, and he felt no need to travel to the third world. He knew nothing about Africa, and didn't really care to.

The next thing Steve knew, he was 6,000 miles from home, in an old Land Rover, on the way to a village. They saw nothing but poverty along the way, yet people smiled and waved.

When they reached the village where they spent the next few days, they couldn't believe how gracious everyone was in the midst of nothing. They were always singing and working together, and often praying. One night, the locals had a special dinner in honor of their guests, and gave them their only chicken. Steve didn't really join in, feeling uneasy with the food, their living conditions, and the overall state of affairs. The villagers took note.

On the last day, before they packed up, Steve spent some time with one of the village elders, helping him with some work. When the time was right, Steve asked him a question. He said, "How can you stand being so poor?" The man stepped back slowly, rubbed his head, and said, "Sir, we are not poor, we just don't have any money." And after a long pause, he said, "As a matter of fact, I was wondering the same thing about you."

WHEN IT'S YOUR TURN

You first help your neighbor, and then she helps her friend
Her friend is so thankful that his smile just won't end.
He goes to the market and sees someone in need
A few simple dollars to fulfill a great deed.
For all throughout time, this rule has stood test:
Give to another and you will be blessed.
It's not about getting when your turn comes around
If you sit there and wait, you will be let down.
Some folks will laugh and dismiss this great plan
They want me to prove it—how sorry I am.
I ask that you try it. As soon as you do
You will see changes—changes in you.
You'll have helped another; this we all know
But something more subtle will begin to show.
Your walk will be straighter, your sky will be bright
A glow from inside you will prove that it's right.
And then when it's your time, have nothing to fear
Your efforts will guide you, and your gifts will appear.

CONSIDERATIONS

1. How can you be a servant in your community without donating money? Who has needs you can meet? Think about your true passions in life, beyond your work. Who can benefit from those skills?

2. Think of a time when you were the recipient of loving service. Name a time when someone selflessly gave of themselves, their talents, or their resources when you needed it most. What organizations or individuals have helped you?

3. Create a dream charity. You don't have to make it happen, but think about it, and make up the foundation or non-profit you'd love to see. Whom do you serve? Who do you want working with you? How much money do you need, and who gives it? You just never know.

TRIPLE DOG DARE

Think of somewhere you would never want to go. Ever. Now contact an organization that serves the most needy people in the heart of this place. Call them and inquire about volunteering for them. Then go do it.

Chapter Seven

Those Who Learn to Fail From History Should Not Be in Charge

"The man who holds the ladder firmly at the bottom is as important as the man on the top." —ANONYMOUS

HELLO, America. How are we? There's something I can't quite put my finger on, but we all notice the tension.

We're at a crossroads, and we've been waiting at the corner of change and complacency for quite some time now. We're battling over going right or left, but that ain't it, so to speak.

Switch on the news or plug into any media outlet and we hear the same recurring themes: frustration, blame, and the desire for a different direction, yet we see the continued inability to make things happen. Sound familiar?

"Life, liberty, and the pursuit of happiness …"

The first Americans worked very hard to craft our nation. What would be the reaction of our Founding Fathers if they watched some of what we call "timely information" for a few hours today? Our political crusades distract us from the deeper issues—something our democratic founders were afraid of. What about our virtues? What about our families? What is liberty? What is freedom? What do we need to do in order to honor these things?

We Americans have more collective similarities than differences. While we squabble about money, news, and leaders, isn't there a bigger picture? Remember the tenets of what makes us truly astounding? When's the last time any of those things rang in our national fabric in a meaningful light? I'm not talking about a positive story about a family or good deed to balance out the negative ones. I mean a true, ongoing representation of how good our society thinks we actually are, down to its core.

As for the news cycle, I have to remind myself that headlines aren't exactly history. They are story captions. At the base of it all, where do "we" and our convictions fit in? You know, the ones that bring us together, and are greater than ourselves? Yep. Here we are.

Headlines and even leaders come and go, but truth always remains. Do you believe that life will improve, "just as soon as that right person gets elected to office?" I think there are many people who truly believe this, and our entire electoral system is built on this idea. Sadly, we suffer for it dearly.

Yes, individual leaders are very important. But are they the only ones who really shape history?

Let's pause and take a look at where we've been.

Our Story

America is one of the most powerful stories in world history. It represents human lives and spiritual hope—everything that makes us unique and strong. It proves that, despite our differences, we are united by timeless truths.

America wrote itself out tyranny. Our Constitution and the Bill of Rights ensure personal liberties and protections—so long as we are willing to claim them.

Throughout history and time, there have been many other wonderful civilizations and lives built as well. They should all be celebrated and learned from.

Our country is based on states, which contain counties, which contain communities and households. So then … we should have leaders based on our laws, not the other way around. The writers set a balance between Congress, the Executive, and the Judiciary. Therefore, we cannot blame any one person or party for our troubles. We're all responsible, and that's a wonderful privilege. It's part of our Constitutional rights to be able to express our opinions. But what are our duties, and where are we in all of this?

Right now, many people feel disappointed with "the system." This will probably always be the case. However, every now and then, we come to a big social turning point where we throw up our hands and shake our heads. "What happened?" we wonder. I believe we are in one of those times right now. Part of it might be related to history, part leadership, but all us. Complacency is a large threat. In the words of Benjamin Franklin, "Only a virtuous people are capable of freedom."

I understand why so many of us want to tune out. It's a heck of a lot easier. But here's the back burner truth: We, the people, have to take this blessing called America and always care for her. The Founders planned for a country that had the ability to peacefully repair itself anytime. Nobody's perfect, but I believe we have the opportunity to do the right thing—if we want to.

If we don't stand for our beliefs, who will?

The "thing" we call news—the voice on the radio, the talking head on television—it's all been said and done. Only the names and faces change. Why do bad things happen again and again? Why do we get so angry over hot topics, but do nothing about them? Why do we re-elect our congressman, despite his poor leadership? So many highs and lows, it feels exhausting. What would happen if we spent all our time focusing on what is right with the world, instead of what's wrong?

History is more than just events to be watched—it's how we move the world, and how we think. It means living. Tomorrow's history will be made by the dreams and efforts we make today. Do we even realize how things have changed? Can you imagine turning on the news all day on a Saturday and just "watching" twenty years ago? That's not exactly leadership.

It doesn't take long to train ourselves to look outside instead of inside for solutions to our problems. In fact, we have built an entire culture on it, and political strategies are one of the most powerful ways we do it.

With regard to our leaders, I believe we need to step back and think about where we are in history: Are they a mirror of us, or are we a mirror of them? Is there even a "them"? Don't they come from "us," the general public?

Our country has always been proud of its ability to think outside the box. Why, then, do we feel so boxed in?

"Oh, but the guys in Washington!" Hear the words, but read between the lines: "I'm mad and don't know what to do with it. I'm disappointed and I feel stuck." What do we really want—and need? Of course we all want people to believe in, leaders who embody the things we hope for.

But looking inward is where the magic lies. We are all leaders. Think of the scoutmaster, the first grade teacher, the volunteer outreach coordinator, and the pastor. Leaders are familiar faces, people who give generously and regularly, with humility. They are the people who make our lives better, because they make things happen. We can count on them, and more important, we can talk to them, and they listen.

Virtuous Leaders and Common Sense

Think of all the great leaders throughout history. The ones who truly changed the world. Rosa Parks, Winston Churchill, Gandhi, *et al.* History presented them with the opportunity, and they stepped into the sands of time. How did they do it? During the Revolutionary War, Congress offered President Washington a $25,000 salary. He rejected it, saying the money was inappropriate, given the state of the nation. He understood that his position was a responsibility, not a reward, and he believed in the fight for his country. What burns inside all of us, making us stand up and change the entire direction of things? Sometimes the circumstances are born from great events, like landing on the moon. Others arise from difficult situations in which true grit is needed, like sitting in the front of that bus. Leadership comes from not accepting the situation as it currently is, and having the forethought and persuasion to get others to follow.

In a speech to Congress, President Lyndon B. Johnson gave his famous "we shall overcome," speech, the phrase borrowed from African American leaders struggling for equal rights. The date was March 15, 1965, a week after deadly racial violence had erupted in Selma, Alabama. Police officers attacked African Americans who were preparing to march to Montgomery in protest of voting rights discrimination. Many of us remember the difficult questions of this era: Could black kids go to school with white kids? Could we work together and live together? In hindsight, we are shocked by those growing pains. How did we manage to move forward? It happened because regular people—real individuals with absolute values—said something.

Johnson's speech is a wonderful one:

I speak tonight for the dignity of man and the destiny of democracy. I urge every member of both parties, Americans of all religions and of all colors, from every section of this country, to join me in that cause.

At times, history and fate meet at a single time in a single place to shape a turning point in man's unending search for freedom. So it was at Lexington and Concord. So it was a century ago at Appomattox. So it was last week in Selma, Alabama. There, long-suffering men and women peacefully protested the denial of their rights as Americans. Many of them were brutally assaulted. One good man—a man of God—was killed.

There is no cause for pride in what has happened in Selma. There is no cause for self-satisfaction in the long denial of equal rights of millions of Americans. But there is cause for hope and for faith in our Democracy in what is happening here tonight. For the cries of pain and the hymns and protests of oppressed people have summoned into convocation all the majesty of this great government—the government of the greatest nation on earth. Our mission is at once the old-est and the most basic of this country—to right wrong, to do justice, to serve man. In our time we have come to live with the moments of great crises. Our lives have been marked with debate about great issues, issues of war and peace, issues of prosperity and depression.

But rarely in any time does an issue lay bare the secret heart of America itself. Rarely are we met with a challenge, not to our growth or abundance, or our welfare or our security, but rather to the values and the purposes and the meaning of our beloved nation. The issue of equal rights for American Negroes is such an issue. And should we defeat every enemy, and should we double our wealth and conquer the stars, and still be unequal to this issue, then we will have failed as a people and as a nation. For with a country, as with a person, "What is a man profited if he shall gain the whole world, and lose his own soul?"

There is no Negro problem. There is no Southern problem. There is no Northern problem. There is only an American problem.

And we are met here tonight as Americans—not as Democrats or Republicans; we're met here as Americans to solve that problem. This was the first nation in the history of the world to be founded with a purpose.

These words make me proud. Yes, it is only a speech given by a controversial elected leader, but it demonstrates real change at work. Johnson reflects on history and asks us to be better people.

Johnson was an old Southern guy. He wasn't particularly admired, nor is he well-loved today, but his was a critical message. Discrimination was a hot potato issue, but we couldn't avoid it any longer. Look carefully and you'll see hearts and minds behind the politics. It was the start of an important countrywide conversation.

If someone asked you to get out a sheet of paper and list the top ten things that make for a powerful leader, what would you write down? I did the exercise myself, and it was a fun but meaningful project. Here's my list.

- Someone who understands that service to others is the highest honor, and believes serving is much better than being served.

- Someone who gives a powerful demonstration of the meaning of the word *character*.

- Someone who is willing to make decisions and stand for something because it is the best thing to do.

- Someone who does not stand down in the face of grueling adversity.

- Someone who lives their life the same way they expect others to live.

- Someone who always remembers where they came from.

- Someone who believes in the rights of those they serve.

- Someone who is loyal, knows how to solve problems, and doesn't make excuses.

- Someone who understands that everything we have and will ever have comes from our creator.

- Someone who truly deserves it.

Why the rant?

So why so much commentary about leadership? And why the drift toward politics? My interest is both personal and professional. I have a strong and emotional pride in our country, and I hope for us to prosper in the future. I want my family and community to have every opportunity for growth and security, but am often stunned by how poorly we lead—and are led—as a nation. I believe things could be much better with our limited number of blessings. There is a great gap between how we regular, hard-working Americans are living our lives and the decisions our leaders are making on our behalf. I believe we need nothing short of a spiritual rebirth, not of leaders, but leadership; one that sets our hearts ablaze with desire.

Leadership is truly a back burner issue.

I am relied upon each day to help others make meaningful life decisions. I act as a guide to maneuver economics and politics for investment purposes, so I have to be up to date with legislation and regulations. It is imperative that I see how politicians affect not only my life, but the lives of the people who trust me to secure their financial futures.

My Parting Thoughts

Our sense of history eludes us these days. The proof is all around us. After all, what are we teaching our children about the history of our country, both bad and good, and what is its emphasis? If we erase certain parts, does it really help them? How long are our investment time frames? Yes, we all say we're in it "for the long haul," but then we go and measure performance by the hour. As we seek to build strong family customs and traditions, how much are we pulling from our elders and the invaluable knowledge they have to share? Do we even want that anymore? And all encompassing, what are we truly learning from our past? When we give our elected leaders the reins, and trust in their abilities to do the right thing, how are their decisions shaping the perpetual strength and legacy of this experiment we call the United States of America?

Our culture is shifting toward valuing the present alone. I believe this is a relatively new phenomenon, and one that will rob us of everything we have. I see the way we're pressing for speed, with technological advancement and exciting invention. It is often difficult to adjust. But when we forget or ignore our past and assume that newer and faster is better, bad things happen. First, our past disappears. Second, we limit the tools available for our society to flourish. And third, our optimism runs out of fuel.

Here's an example:

For many generations in this country, debt was not looked upon as a positive thing, nor was it excessive at the personal, corporate, or government level. Imagine if everyone had been in debt up to their ears during the Great Depression? Over time, and especially recently, our attitude toward debt has significantly changed on virtually all fronts, including social acceptability, corporate growth, and government policy. I study economics and finance for a living, and often find myself in disconnect over what I thought I knew, and what has become "normal." We now live in a world where there is one debt gear: full speed ahead.

So what has changed?

I believe that one of the most pressing issues of our time, at least financial and political, is the long-term debt and accumulated obligations of our country. They represent many things, but at the core is a discussion about leadership. For many years, our frugality was the backbone of our character. Today, the place we are in represents a tragedy, and the silence is deafening. What kind of inheritance does that leave our children? Talk about legacy.

Thomas Jefferson once said, "The maxim of buying nothing without the money in our pockets to pay for it makes our country one of the happiest on earth ... I place economy among the first and most important of Republican virtues, and public debt as the greatest of the dangers to be feared."

Think out fifty years from now. What do you think the national debt will be? How do you think the children being born today will be affected by it? How do you think debt will be accepted culturally and socially? What is our current want and ability to see things through?

I want to emphasize the role of our leaders. Above all, good leadership requires an understanding of what is important about our past, and what needs to be done in the present, in order to create a strong and meaningful future. I believe this quality has been lost and needs to be restored.

There are many things going on in this world, which are representative of how we are not only failing to learn, but learning to fail from history. As we think about those who lead us, whether it be in government, faith, or family, let's give some thought to how our history plays a part in what we all become. Anyone with a lesser perspective should not be in charge.

L I B E R T Y

Over two hundred years
since our country commenced.
A light for the world,
there's been none like it since.
So what makes her different?
The pursuit, is what I say.
Of life and of happiness
may liberty show the way.
Please don't confuse me
—perfection I do not claim.
Our history is filled
with hurt and with shame.
But the vision and forethought
our founders prescribed.
Is worth our defending,
and why so many died.
There are those who'll attack us
from outside and within.
Are they scared of our freedom?
Are they free from our sin?
With an eye on future,
what changes should stand?
Common sense again bless us
and faith heal our land.
To define this great nation,
a task which is broad.
There's one thing for certain—
we're one under God.

CONSIDERATIONS

1. Who is your favorite leader of all time?

2. Read the Constitution and the Bill of Rights. What three things stand out to you? How are they reflected in your daily life? How do these documents inspire your values?

3. What is your favorite era of American history? Why? If you could time travel and visit for a week, what would you want to do?

TRIPLE DOG DARE

Think about how leadership has been crucial to the outcomes of conflicts we have had in the past and will have in the future. How can the decisions you make affect history?

Chapter Eight

Dis-Ease

AS I was putting together the chapters for this book, one topic kept coming up over and over again. While it is a subject that hits close to home with everyone, it is something extremely difficult to discuss. The subject is our health.

Health (along with religion, which is coming up next) touches all aspects of our lives. We may be discussing our health 24 hours a day in this country, but there is a lot of confusion around the issue.

This chapter is an emotional one, but I know you can handle it. My own buttons are being pushed as well. Please know that none of this is a sermon, nor is it medical advice. It's reality. We're all in this together. We have to hold one another accountable. Change is a beautiful thing.

The Camping Trip

Sally had been looking forward to spending time with her dad for the last several months. When planning their annual dad/daughter weekend, they decided that this year they wanted to go camping in the mountains of Colorado. A few days of fresh air, wildlife, and time together was much anticipated. Sally loved her father with her whole heart, and had waited all year to spend time with him.

They arrived in Denver and drove a few hours to a national park—it was even more beautiful than they had anticipated. On the morning of the third day, Sally woke early to get things in order. The clear sky was sapphire blue, with a dozen birds chatting in the trees overhead. She got dressed for the day, careful not to make noise, and curiously watched a chipmunk race around the trunk of an aspen. After a bit, she went back to the tent to wake her father. She tapped on the nylon, but got no response. She sensed that there was something wrong, "Dad?" she whispered. There was no reply. "Dad?"

She unzipped the front and saw him lying still in his olive-green sleeping bag. She stared for a moment. It *doesn't look right*, she thought. *He's very, very pale.*

He's gone.

Sally screamed and grabbed her cell phone. She called 911 and waited for help. She sat by the ashes of last night's campfire and rocked back and forth until the emergency crew arrived. Time stopped for this fifteen-year-old girl.

His death was a shock, but not surprising. There's more to the story.

For several years, Sally's dad ignored his health. As the CEO at a large company, his bottom lines came first, meaning he had no balance between work and home. He struggled with high blood pressure, he was overweight, and he suffered regular headaches, but he still carried on as if this was completely acceptable. He'd take a pill or have a drink and return to his to-do lists. The camping trip itself had been delayed twice because he wasn't feeling well. There was always an excuse, something to distract him. No matter what trouble he was having, he was back to work early the next morning.

After a series of fainting spells, he was diagnosed with severe diabetes. "Everyone has diabetes," he quipped, and he continued to push himself. He lived with worsening pain, but refused to get help. Truthfully, he didn't want to admit the gravity of his situation, and he didn't want to appear weak. He was the man of the family and needed control. He was the one who made things happen.

The point of this story is not to say how anyone should live their lives, but to explore the relationship between the decisions we make, what is important to us, and the legacies we build.

Everything is connected

Each of us is at a certain stage in life. We may be getting ready to retire, or we may be twenty years out. Maybe we are dealing with aging parents, or the loss of a lifemate and best friend. Perhaps we're preparing for the wedding of a child or shifting into the gear of being a grandparent for the first time. It's the stuff we dream about and measure our lives by. In the planning that we do, health is at the center of the discussion, at least indirectly. We either assume that we will be in good health when we participate in these activities, or we plan what to do in case we are not. But how do we think about our health, what does our culture say about it, and how does it shape our lives?

In the interest of tying things together, let's do a recap:

- **Chapter One: Money, it's time for you to know—** We are encouraged to think about the things that are most important to us, and what we value. My guess is if you had to name your top five things, your health would be on the list. Health is not just about "diet and exercise," but is also financial, intellectual, spiritual, and emotional.

- **Chapter Two: Before the day after—**We all know we are going to die someday, but we live in a world that seeks to skirt around this, at least super-ficially. I believe in living life with a comfortable understanding that this road we are on only hap-pens once, yet we are eternal. There is life and then there is death. Health is everything that happens in between.

- **Chapter Three: Talk to your parents**—Elder care is one of the most important and complex issues facing our country today. Our preparation for our later years encompasses money, family, time, societal structure, and living arrangements. Talking about this and planning for it are critical.

- **Chapter Four: Precious time**—This one asks you not only to think about how you spend your time, but also to examine how you think about food. After all, we are what we eat. Think back to the time when sharing a meal was the centerpiece of our days, rather than a footnote to them. Think about not only how different the food we eat today is, but the stress we are creating for ourselves.

- **Chapter Five: Dude, let's buy a castle**—"Live life to the fullest and ask questions later" is the theme of this chapter. We've all heard stories of people who narrowly escape death and then live their lives in a new way. I encourage all of us to live life to the fullest, before large and difficult things happen. What we think about determines what becomes of us, and health is central to this, both physically and mentally.

• **Chapter Six: Serving yourself and serving humanity**—I have always had a special place in my thoughts and prayers for those who struggle in society. Among the poor, health is often one of the key concerns. How we treat the least among us is one of the underlying determinates of the health of a nation, and the health benefits of serving others can also be numerous.

• **Chapter Seven: Those who learn to fail from history should not be in charge**—More and more over time, the trend has been to look to our elected leaders to help shape society. Recently, we had one of the bitterest conflicts in leadership in our nation's history; it had to do with how we deliver health care to our citizens. I'm not talking about the product, but the process. Whatever your thoughts, we have chosen our path. Now we will live out our decision, and it will affect everyone. But no matter what, always remember that when someone asks you who your primary care provider is, you should tell them that it is you.

Some background on me: A few years ago, I was at dinner with some friends. It was a relaxing get-together with drinks, appetizers, and giant entrées—a fun night out. During the evening, I noticed that my good friends Max and Suzanne had refrained from drinking much and ordered only a light dinner. This caught my interest, as the rest of us were busy "living it up." So I asked them about it. Max said, "I just buried my friend last week. Before he died, he gave me a copy of a book that he said that he wished he'd received earlier, because it might have saved his life."

Wow! That's a dinner conversation I don't usually have. I told him I would put it on my reading list, and went back to my delectable dinner.

I have always been fairly sensible when it comes to diet and health. I grew up knowing that exercise was important. I thought I was eating well. I will admit that I always seemed to have a few pounds to lose, but what the heck—you only live once, right? Moreover, I had an Italian grandmother standing by at the table, always telling me to clean my plate. That kind of stuff stays with you. All the while, I've always had an interest in human health. Like many people, I've been confused about what to do and whom to trust. Protein, carbs, cholesterol, gluten, no gluten—after a while, it all sounds the same. Most of us have access to good information, but it is very hard to know what to do with it all.

So I ordered a book called *The China Study*. It was a history of food in America, a detailed study on the relationship between nutrition and disease, where we stand today, and much more. I had never encountered anything quite like it. I was happy to receive it, angry at our "system," and motivated to learn more. Why didn't they teach this stuff in schools? Why is it so hidden? I wanted more.

I found out that one of the authors was a professor at Cornell University, so I contacted the school to see if there was anything else I could do. They said he had some online classes starting soon, and I signed up. So for many months thereafter, I would bring my dinner to work, and after client meetings I went to school. I completed the training and am now certified in plant-based nutrition. I linked health to two very important topics during this experience: trust and responsibility.

As I look back, the driving force behind my desire to learn more about nutrition and disease was my family. When it comes to eating, I would say we were a typical family unit. My parents, uncles, cousins, and grandparents—we all deal with disease, emotional eating, bad habits, stubbornness, and a whole host of other things. I ate what my parents ate, and my parents ate what *their* parents ate. When things go wrong, we blame it on genetics. At a traditional gathering or vacation, we load up on "fun" food because we think we deserve it. Then we spend the rest of the time talking about how big we feel and how we are trying to lose weight. We chat about surgery, who has cancer, skin growths, all of it. It all seems so normal, despite the fact that it's insane!

For the past decade or so, I have been learning everything I can about food, nutrition, disease, and health—and
how they all relate. How much of it can I personally manage?
I've come to a couple of conclusions. First, no one will ever
care more about your health than you. Second, I have found
that good nutrition is the absolute key to life. Hippocrates, the
father of western medicine, said, "Let food be thy medicine,
and medicine be thy food."

When you think about health in America, what comes to
mind? Is it health care? How about the news reports remind-
ing us daily that we are the sick and fat, and that we lead the
world in cancer and disease? Wait, maybe it's the commercials
talking about the best way to achieve weight loss or healthy
eating. Or are you thinking about it from a spiritual, well-
being point of view? Whatever you may be pondering, I hope
you can agree that the subject of health is deep and wide (no
pun intended). It affects our pocket book, our relationships
with other people, and even reaches into freedom and dignity.

How come it's so hard to figure out what to do regarding
what we eat, and how to care for ourselves? Why has there
been such a gigantic rise in disease in such a relatively short
period of time in America? Why do television commercials
tell us to talk to our doctors about a certain condition or
medication instead of our doctors telling us about it? Why
don't schools teach us about nutrition, with surgery and medicine as backups? How did we get to the point where the

average American consumes a half pound of sugar every day? Why does the cost of health care keep rising to unsustainable levels? How did separating from our parents as they age and sending them off to be cared for by other people become the norm, not the exception? How about the trend of being sick for the last ten to twenty years of our lives, and thinking this is just what happens when we get old? Our food quality, distribution system, and consumption patterns have changed dramatically. Is it better? You get the point. I guess what I'm saying is, are we okay with all of this? Health used to be easier. It wasn't a topic of conversation or strategy; it just was. Now it's a separate and distinct "being" from ourselves. It is a market, and as a sector it represents a good portion of the annual gross domestic product of America. By the way, you know the answers to these questions. My question is, why do we find ourselves having to ask ourselves these questions?

I have never met anyone who didn't want to be as healthy as they can be. Yet taking care of ourselves is becoming harder and harder. Look at the amount of time and money we spend on health, versus our actual state of health. On the surface, we are all moving along, going about our lives, living in the world like this is the best time in history. Yet, when we slow down a bit, we see a different story. When it comes down to it, we see stress. Lots of it. It's the new rite of passage.

For some people, health can be a representation of life's ultimate fairness or unfairness. Why do some people get sick and others don't? Who should be able to tell you how to treat your sickness, or wellness for that matter? Who should pay for it? These are big issues.

When I put together a full-blown financial plan for our clients, there are many moving parts at play. We look at how much money is currently accumulated, investment returns over time, inflation, income needs, what to do with the money as it is passed on, how time will be spent, and so on. The thing with the single greatest impact on what the plan eventually looks like is how long the people live, and what their health is going to be like. When we transition to a time in life when we must leave our homes and receive care, money is a huge issue, and emotions run high.

When someone in our family is struck with a life-threatening health situation, everything else in life stops. Everything. When Mom dies, and you are wandering aimlessly through her home, contemplating the work you have in front of you, it is there when you stop and realize what life is all about.

I believe that it is during these times in our lives when we are given the most grace, and perhaps redemption. But honestly, they can present opportunities to make mistakes that can haunt us for a lifetime. Even though we often feel like we are trying to shoot at a moving target, doing our best to align our expectations is something that can do wonders. It also changes the discussion from "how is my health" to "what are those important things I want to live for?"

Remember when you were ten years old? You didn't think about diet and health. You didn't think about "the end." You only considered tomorrow. What freedom it was, to run with the wind and feel at home in your own little body.

There is an old saying that we spend our health accumulating our wealth, and then spend our wealth trying to keep our health. If we stepped back a bit, and took to heart that our health is part of our wealth, we probably wouldn't see the need to pound ourselves into the ground working so hard. We also wouldn't need a world of other people trying to give us their version of "solutions" to every aspect of our lives, because they would take care of themselves. Throw that stone in the water and let it start making some ripples, why don't you?

Here's another story:

Remember Sally, whose father died while camping? Sally's best friend was Hannah. Hannah's father was in a car accident that left him in a wheelchair. He lost his job and suffered terrible pain; the family had no insurance, and he spent months in an exhausting rehab facility. Life can be unfair. You'd think that Hannah and Sally had a lot in common then—they both endured tragedies involving their fathers. Think again! After some time of surrender and prayer, Hannah's father was able to make a remarkable transition. He knew that things would never be the same, but he embraced the changes with fierce gratitude. "Poor me!" became "It could've been much worse!" and he became a completely different man. He is more active and available than ever before. He "made lemonade" with his new reality, and became a reliable father who really knew his family. They lived within their means for the very first time, meaning that he worked smarter and not harder in a new consultant position. He spent time drawing, cooked with his kids, and took a leadership role with in the family's church. The old father, fully able to walk, could never have gone so far!

Let's think about health in a new way.

Do you want to remain independent as long as possible, or walk your daughter down the aisle? Think of the reasons you want to be strong. Clear away all the things that distract you, and let the things that are meaningful to you slowly move into your life. Be honest with yourself. You have a spiritual, emotional, physical, and a financial meaning in this world, so don't for one minute minimize the importance of your presence. There is nothing that could ever replace the wonder that is you.

THE WAITRESS

James, his wife, Annie, and their three children
were out of town for a fun weekend.
Hungry for lunch, they decided to stop
by an old-style cafe named "Ginger's Place,"
which looked adorable.
They dreamed of the ice cream sundaes
and old-fashioned burgers. They parked and raced in.

After they sat down, it took ten minutes for them to
be greeted, and the place didn't seem that busy.
When they were recognized, the waitress
didn't say hello. She basically threw their
silverware down and walked away. No water.
They looked at one another,
and wondered what they had done.

Ten minutes later, she came back and asked
if they were ready. She rudely took their order
and walked away. At this point James was
re-thinking their small-town quest,
and Annie was discounting her tip.

When their food arrived, much of it was wrong,
but the waitress was gone before they could say anything.
By the time they got her, the food was cold,
and she really didn't seem to care.

Dis-Ease

Just then, their six-year-old, Olivia, said,
"Ma'am, this is a very nice place you have, and you are pretty.
Are you mad at us, or is something wrong? You look sad."
In that instant, a tear formed in the eye of the waitress,
and she let out a huge sigh.
She explained that she had just lost her husband,
and was having a very hard time with it.
She genuinely apologized for not having done
a very good job, and escaped back to the kitchen
before the tears really came rolling down.

James looked at his family with a feeling of guilt,
but also a sense of pride in his six-year-old daughter.
In a split second, she had reminded an entire restaurant
of one of life's basic rules. Nothing more was said.

As they finished their ice cream,
paid their bill, and turned to leave,
little Olivia approached the waitress.
She hugged her, leaned into her ear, and said,
"Everything will be all right.
You are pretty, and you have a very nice place."

CONSIDERATIONS

1. Take a day off before you get sick. Refresh, renew, recharge, putter, breathe, do laundry, go to a museum … be a human being.

2. Keep a photo of yourself as a child on your bathroom mirror or in a wallet, somewhere you will regularly see it. Ask him what he needs. Take care of her.

3. What health habits did you learn from your parents? How have they affected the way you live your life?

TRIPLE DOG DARE

Think about all of the different ways that health comes into play in your life. Write them down and make the connections between them. What have been the hard things? What can you do to align your expectations to be better prepared? Where are your successes?

Chapter Nine

"Never Let the Failure of Man Determine Your Relationship with God."

THEY say we must believe in something greater than ourselves, something that gives us perspective and motivation. Is that the same as our morals and values? Are they enough?

No matter what the road of life brings in this world, is it just over at the end? Some believe so. I do not. The way we practice our morals depends on belief, and I make the claim that success in that venture hangs on faith. It is faith that connects the dots of our back burner chapters, and that is the topic I wish to close with.

We talk about our money, but what of the spiritual emptiness that often lies behind the want? We try very hard not to talk about death. We quit going to church because of this or that. Serving our fellow man easily fades away. We walk away from a family relationship forever over one argument. All these issues are spiritual at their core. Even a life very well-lived brings challenges to the discussion of eternal meaning.

From whose perspective are we living?

Building the perfect lives for ourselves in this world can be very rewarding, and can keep us quite occupied. But if true success were as easy as getting a job promotion or moving to a nicer house, wouldn't you think there would be some seriously fulfilled people by now?

Faith provides an opportunity for a very different view of success. It tells us that all these back burner topics are symptoms, not the actual problem. When we inch away from faith, it's easy to fill the space with all these distracting issues. But what about the deeper meaning that provides true joy?

My relationship with God is fundamental. I struggle with the burner issues, but God is the actual stove.

I learned about joy from the Missionaries of Charity Sisters in Haiti, who run and keep a home for dying children. These women have given up all worldly goods and ambitions in order to dedicate their lives to serving God by comforting the poor. There they are, in one of the poorest places on the planet, working arduously with absolute joy. It isn't easy, what they do; it is emotionally and physically taxing work—outright labor. But they move through the day with purpose and passion. They do what they do because of their faith. All the distractions of the world fade away when you spend time in their presence. Their simplicity is something I yearn for; they aren't in the least bit concerned with money, family drama, competitive neighbors, computers, or Pilates. Their lives cut straight to the point: service, love, and people. At the center of it all: God.

Mother Teresa founded the Missionaries of Charity. Her life is a vital illustration of my point. I can't imagine what it was like for her to feel the calling into service, leaving Albania for India. She did it because of her faith, and she understood that her belief would take care of all the unknown variables. This can, of course, be very uncomfortable. And just because we have a solid relationship with God doesn't mean that things will be easy.

Mother Teresa struggled profoundly during her life. It's well known that she suffered from depression and doubt. But she labored on, doing ugly work in a most beautiful way. But she kept going, focused with love and intention, and defined success in a new, modern way.

This is the lesson: She was by no means perfect, but she did everything in her power to prosper the lives of the poor, and she committed with her whole heart. She let nothing get in the way of her love for God. She was wholly focused on God's direction and gave herself absolutely.

Today, her religious order consists of over 4,600 sisters and is active in 133 countries. They run hospices and homes for people with HIV/AIDS, leprosy, and tuberculosis. They run soup kitchens, dispensaries, mobile clinics, children's and family counseling programs, orphanages, and schools. Members adhere to vows of chastity, poverty, and obedience ... and a fourth vow, to give "wholehearted free service to the poorest of the poor."

Mother Teresa was awarded the Nobel Peace Prize in 1979. In 2003, she was beatified as "Blessed Teresa of Calcutta."

Of course most of us don't have those kinds of extreme life situations. But how can we stay true to ourselves and our word in a man-made world?

I grew up in a "typical" American Catholic family. Religion was part of our upbringing, and we went to church together nearly every Sunday. I attended Catholic school until the eighth grade, after which my parents gave us a personal choice between public and private high school. The other kids didn't have to wear uniforms, and they got home earlier than us, so it was an obvious choice. We made our decision and left our old friends behind. At the new school, we met many other good people. Altogether, it was a positive experience. I still attended Mass on Sundays (usually), even after those late Saturday nights on the town—I was a true high-school knucklehead.

As I look back on the role of faith in my early years, I am deeply grateful. I learned the golden rule, studied the timeless lessons of the Bible, had good people to look up to, and understood that I was created specifically by God. But some vivid memories pressed me in a direction that made my journey much longer than it needed to be.

I recall my parents saying that they never really got anything out of going to Mass. They'd say, "I can't understand what the priest is saying" because of his foreign accent. We always went to church, but I never quite understood why. Attendance seemed more like a task than a celebration. There always seemed to be something to complain about. I got the faith thing; that God loved me, but I had too many human questions. I was confused. It was a classic case of "do as I say, not as I do." And because formative years are an important time to model spiritual behavior, much of my curiosity and discipline slowly went out the window.

As I entered my college years, I was drawn away from the Catholic faith, and quit going to Mass on weekends. Somewhere along the line, I was introduced to a non-denominational church, which I attended for several years. It seemed to be a direct answer to some of the things about my Catholic experience that upset me. It felt much more welcoming, and addressed my emotional real-life issues at the time. There was much more singing, and lots of standing up and moving of the hands (which completely freaked me out). It helped me find fellowship and explore old faith issues in new ways. It served to validate all of my previous frustrations.

And then I met Maggie.

When I met my wife, I was just starting to come off the high that my new non-denominational life was providing.

Here she was, a gorgeous girl from Omaha, the youngest of eight, and extremely Catholic. She was—and is—the real deal. Maggie went to Catholic school from cradle to diploma and was someone very special, very strong. As we moved along in our relationship, we had some faith-relationship speed bumps. Maggie trusted in things that I found frustrating. If we went out of town for the weekend, her priority was to find a place for Mass. I would say, "We are on vacation, what's the big deal?" She'd reply, "What does that have to do with it? Mass is Mass. Priorities, darling."

Over time, I must admit, I was drawn back into a way of life that had once provided a strange sense of comfort. I knew what it was like to attend regular services and give commitment. Yet at the same time, my vexation seemed to grow. It was like I was using all of my past excuses to prevent myself from experiencing what was most intimate to me in my life: my faith. In the middle of this developing intimacy with another human being, I was diving into a much more meaningful place. I felt vulnerable and wary, because I was being asked to make decisions about the two most personal aspects of my life. It was a weird deal, and I couldn't explain it.

A few years later, we were married, and we bought a new home together in a small river town. We found a local church, and just as we joined, it received a new pastor. Over time, we became more and more involved, and we made some won-derful friends in the process.

My journey back to the Catholic faith was in full force, and planning our traditional wedding together allowed me to see and appreciate parts of the faith that I had never known before, even after attending church hundreds or thousands of times in my life.

One day I was having coffee with our priest, as we often did on Saturday mornings. We got into a discussion about faith-based topics. I was complaining about the whole priest scandal, among other things. I finally said, with a little anger in my voice, "How do you think I feel?" Father paused, then looked me directly in the eye and said, "How do you think I feel? Lee, never let the failure of man determine your rela-tionship with God."

This simple sentence changed my view of religion for-ever. Until that point, I felt that religion was in some ways all about me—my comfort, my struggle, my thinking, and my hope for the future. It never quite sank through my dense head that it was the workings of the world at large. Faith is timeless, personal, and cultural, and surely I was not the first person to question a particular system. While many of us are frustrated about things as we relate to faith, these "things" are not about faith at all, but about us.

Here and Now

As we look at the world today, religion seems to be having a tough time. Many people seem to be frustrated with their faith. Some are exasperated because it seems like their faith doesn't work in the modern world, that it is old-fashioned or out of date. Some, as I mentioned before, are mad at the organization of their faith; the structure. It also appears that our culture is becoming more and more secular. Churches and schools are closing all around us. It's like our culture is giving us an excuse to remove faith from our lives, and it's all made very convenient.

We are watching religion dwindle. Why are we giving up so easily?

Some folks say that they are religious, but just don't like "organized religion." Virtually everything in our society is organized in some manner. Neighborhoods, schools, government, families, clubs, sports—everything. So why do we put our stick in the ground so firmly about the "organized" part of faith? What do we do about "organized cable," which fills our lives with garbage? We remove God from our lives. But subtracting God (as if He might be subtracted!) causes things to crumble. Things fall apart, and we wonder why. When the spiritual trust goes, then the organized parts of our lives begin to falter. Then we blame God, and leave the organized part. Instead of being mad at God, why don't we stick together, abide by his rules, and ask him to bless our lives and heal our land?

Oh, did I say that out loud? We can try to run away, but there's really nowhere to go. We can't get away from the one who created us.

As I noted earlier, church attendance in the United States is extremely low. There is much infighting among faiths, not only regarding the larger concept of faith, but with newborn cultural issues. We see this largely in the Christian belief system, with so many factions and sects. Depending on where you get your facts, there are between 30,000 and 40,000 denominations in the world, and that's just Christians.

So many of today's news clashes are religion-based. In cultures all over the globe, we see war and trauma. Certainly, there are people who have an opinion about God! So where do we stand? Take away all the wars, fighting, and scandals, and we are still individuals with personal spiritual questions. We make mistakes. But we cannot afford to think that the answers lie here, on Earth.

By no means do I mean to say that we shouldn't hold religious leaders and trends accountable; there are some terrible thing happening in the name of faith! What looks proper to one faith may be horrid to another. I lived for many years with deep anger toward the church I'm now committed to. It's been a valuable educational experience to come around again, asking questions and making deliberate choices. The challenges have made me a thousand times stronger.

Maybe it is just the human condition, or perhaps the course of history.

We all have to believe in something, right? Or else nothing fundamentally matters, and we come apart at the seams. Where do you think we are right now, at this moment in history as it relates to faith? Why were you born when you were? Was it random? Or perfect?

In the end, it doesn't prove beneficial to create human distractions for our spiritual problems. The values on which we base all our decisions—how did we get them in the first place? Before the Constitution, before etiquette books, good intentions, and family ideals—we had the Ten Commandments. We have ways of living that were given to us for spiritual reasons. Everything we should do—and shouldn't do—is spelled out in a list of instructions that have timeless universal beginnings.

Whatever your situation, and whatever you believe, the culmination of everything you are and everything you build will be directly tied to your legacy.

In accumulation, we can lose everything. We can lose every single thing! All the stuff, all the goodies, and all the titles will fall. Our faith remains. The world can do all sorts of bad things to us, and we can let it. Or we can adopt a different mindset and live with our hearts wide open. It's a choice. There are always going to be bad people and poor people and human struggles. However, no one is ever going to convince me that going it alone is a better strategy than having the creator of the universe on your team.

I understand that we are now living in a world in which it is becoming increasingly difficult for people to talk about their faith. My question is … so what? What do you think faith is? What are you going to do about it?

Stand up for your life like your faith depends on it...*because it does!*

Stand up for your faith like your life depends on it...*because someday it will!*

FAITH

There are in this world
Two ways life to lead.
Some people search for proof
And others simply believe.
To explore a definition
Or hold it tangibly
Is by its very nature
An extreme anomaly.
There's something deep inside us;
It guides us on our road
When we let go completely,
That's when it truly shows.
Faith—where does it come from?
It comes from in the soul.
Believe is all we have to do;
Release thy own control.
Next time you feel you're searching
And don't know where to turn,
Lift your eyes up to the clouds
And know your thoughts are heard.
When peace surrounds your body
It's then and there you'll know,
That everything will be all right—
Your faith has told you so.

CONSIDERATIONS

1. What were you taught about faith from the time you were a child until today? How has it changed?

2. Think about any frustrations you have had in your life about faith or religion. What are they? Are they about the faith itself, or about people?

3. What leaders in your life have made the most difference for you? If they are still with us, go tell them.

4. Where do you go for solace and quiet reflection? How can you do more listening, more questioning, and more searching?

TRIPLE DOG DARE

Give your faith a chance.

Chapter Ten

On the Front Burner

FOR every book, there is a writer and a reader. It is a very special relationship that allows for honesty and the exchange of ideas. This connection is intimate, as you've allowed me to climb into your head and heart for a while. It has been an exciting journey, to say the least, and also the fulfillment of a lifelong dream. I am grateful for the time we have spent together.

As a "student of the world," a devotee of writing, and someone who has spent my entire adult life talking to people about values, I feel I've been given a unique combination of ideas to share.

Throughout human history, among the billions who have lived, each of us has a unique set of circumstances. One thing that has not changed, however, is that we are here, and are presented with the things that make life what it is. Time keeps moving, but we are still at the center. Until we completely screw it up for ourselves, or until further notice from above, this is the way it is going to be.

We live in an interesting time. We confront topics as broad as varying belief systems, as powerful as deciding our geopolitical future, and as close to home as how we choose to educate our children. We are constantly bombarded with marketing from virtually every industry in existence, attempting to shape our view of what we should be. Things are moving so quickly, and we are pressed with so many demands, that the world of today is going to make the historians of the future wince. However, I feel we are just getting started. It is truly my belief that when we gain an understanding of these things, among many others, we will see just how the items in the previous chapters have come to pass. These important topics are not just issues, but intersections.

It turns out that the directions we take are just as important.

In some ways, it feels like we are the proverbial frog in a pot who doesn't know he is sitting in cooking water until it is too late. Perhaps we have been distracted by our new culture of instant gratification, and we don't see the dangers lurking. If we stop for a moment, we see the pot on the stove and notice the heat of the water. Reality can be jarring. Denial keeps us paralyzed. It's like cognitive dissonance and normalcy bias combined.

So what?

We can continue complaining about money, stress, and schedules and say the world is nuts and there's not a thing we can do about it. Or we can admit that we need to take a step back, define what is most important to us, and live our lives with dedication to those things. Just imagine … the results will be amazing. It will help us get back to a more meaningful style of living. This is powerful stuff.

The premise of this book is that there is a gap between what we say is most important to us and how we are currently living our societal lives. The solution is meant to be personal, and possibly as unique as the reader. My ultimate desire is for us to start a blazing discussion in our hearts, with our families, and in our communities about one simple thing—us.

The hardest part of writing this book was to give it a serious slant while maintaining an optimistic outlook; it was difficult for me to express in words how our challenges can be opportunities. After all, how does one spend so much time in difficult themes without gaining some kind of wayward attitude? The truth is that the intention scripted from this author's pen is with unwavering certainty toward a bright future, one filled with blessings and grace. *Otherwise, I wouldn't have bothered.*

You must believe it's possible, too, my friend, or you would not have made it this far.

And so it is with our lives. Let's all pay attention to the

signs in the road and make the appropriate adjustments. You and I are free to enjoy this world, to seize the beauty we have been given. Let us all remove the fear from our hearts and our minds. And most important, always remember, it's just life. Your life!

Now let's turn on that front burner and get those discussions cooking!

All my best, and thank you so much for taking the time.

—Lee

BREAD FOR THE JOURNEY

ADVICE

There's something I've noticed good folks sharing with me.
They say I can take it or leave it; it's free.
It deals with my life, and how it should be
Based on their view; (their perception of me).
The more I accomplish, the faster it comes
As if my life has problems and their lives have none.
Do you know of these critics I've been telling about?
They prey on your feelings and fill you with doubt.
Well, to this dilemma I've created a tool
To keep me on track—let me share it with you.
I tell them my life is not mistake free
But the road that I travel is how I want it to be.
That I trust in decisions which were already made
And I look to a future which is yet to be paved.
The life that we live is so hard on its own
Their rear-view suggestions I do not condone.
For what I am asking please look and you'll see
I'm not being perfect; I'm just being me.

"ALL I NEED TO KNOW IN LIFE, I LEARNED IN CHURCH"

Be on time. If you come late, you either
have to sit in the very front or very back.
Getting involved in things and helping out
is better than just sitting there.
If you do something often enough,
it becomes a habit and you want more of it.
You may not agree with everything someone says,
but you should at least stay awake and listen to them.
It's not success, but often forgiveness
that is the key to life.
Exploring what exists beyond yourself
keeps everything in perspective.
If you just look around, there is always someone
very close by who needs you.
Taking a day to rest is a really good idea.
Looking someone in the eye and shaking their hand
builds a sense of trust, and even community.
If you do something one day, and then don't live the same way
the rest of the week, it never really works out.
The rules of life are simple, but not easy.
Some people have really bad singing voices,
but if they truly enjoy it, what the heck?
We are all very different,
but there will always be things we have in common.
We should focus on those things.
Honoring that to which we are committed means everything.
Never let the failure of man determine your relationship with God.

BLESSINGS

How can we tell
when we have been blessed
When the lives that we lead
are so full of unrest?
To travel this further,
one thing must be known:
We're all given blessings;
there's none left alone.
When you pray, hope, or wish
for something you need
Blessings don't live here;
they're reserved for other deeds.
Wishes are granted.
Prayers are answered.
Our hopes are what's wanted,
but blessings are planted.
Look into the mirror
and reflect on your days
And the things you've been given
in so many ways.
When nothing is happening
(at least in your eyes)
Not to worry my friends,
it's the kind in disguise.
So now I must leave you
until another time
Be thinking of your blessings;
I just counted mine.

CHILDREN

Tell me …
What is more precious
than little children?
They can teach you
more than college.
They can test your limits
And fill your mind.
They're complex,
but they keep it simple.
They're honest.
They're interested in life,
So much that they glow.
Children love themselves,
And they love others
Just because …
Children smile a lot.
They tell you their secrets
And confide in you.
Not only are they
An abundance of love in themselves;
They bring out the best in us.
Listen to children
Teach children
Learn from children
Believe in children
Love children
One day,
They will give you the greatest gift of all.
They will thank you!

CONTENTMENT

How do you measure all that you've gained
Do you start with your assets and the status you reign?
If this is your vision, so much left to do
There's bigger, there's better, and it's all just for you.
We're sharing a season where work is our core
Because this means we're happy, and happy means more.
We've forgotten the basics. We're unsure of our role.
It's drowning our spirit and it's piercing our soul.
The greatest of blessings in the days that we live
Is to know we have plenty and there's room left to give.
With this, please remember to measure your life
But subtract your possessions and your math will be right.
So now it's your moment … what will you choose?
Those earthly belongings or the ones you can't lose?

D E S T I N Y

In each of our days we come to expect
The direction and meaning our lives will project.
Not always, but often, things go as we like.
These decisions, we made them; they have to be right.
But then come the hard times, they were not in the plan.
How could this even happen, our emotions demand.
When confronting these moments just what do you do?
Blame life and curse others or search for the clues?
When the load becomes heavy, that's when we must grow
If not for our trials, what good would we know?
One thing for the reader; a thought to peruse
Who closes that window and which door will we choose?
In each of our troubles are the moon and the stars
But the hard part is knowing which decisions are ours.
Knowing all in this season could mean nothing the next
For it's not just the reason, but the entire context.
So sharpen your vision, but leave yourself room
Because just when you're certain your destiny looms.
It's not where we're going or how we get there
But the meaning it brings us through the lives that we share.

FREEDOM

We're born in this world
With nothing to lose.
But as we grow older
There's a change in our views.
Religion and culture,
Careers, speech, and law;
We feel we are limited—
"Surrounded by walls."
A thread, though, weaves through us
The need to be free;
To pursue all we're able
A right granted thee.
If your freedom was taken
Then you would know,
What it means to be stripped
Of your person; your soul.
Opportunity for one
Not outcome for all.
This misunderstanding
Our clearest downfall.
Our country was formed
On debate, risk, and God
To carry on liberty
This is our job.
An ode to our founders
No compromise et al.
Freedom for one
And freedom for all.

GIVE

Did you ever notice
How good it is to help another?
The happiness always runs deeper,
When giving than when receiving.
Could you imagine
Living your life in that state?
Why can't you?
I firmly believe
That if you trust in yourself
But also focus wholeheartedly,
On the success of those around you,
You will never have to worry
About your own achievements.
They will take care of themselves.
They say you must leave the shore
To see the beauty of the harbor.
This way of life can seem
Against the nature of things at first.
But actually, there isn't a better way.
Life runs in a constant circle.
You can either be a meaningful part
And reap the meaningful benefits,
Or stand alone, and always wonder
Why life is so hard.

GROUNDED

One foot on the ground,
and one in the air;
It appears so exciting,
but rarely compares.
To have both feet
planted securely below
Is a gift only those
who achieve it will know.
Chance, risk, and adventure
appeal to the sense
But the results become after
a flurry of emptiness.
Structure and balance, not
attractive at all?
At least you will know
where you stand when you fall.
If you can't enjoy
a walk in the park
Then how will escape
fill up your heart?

If you see a situation
that is better than yours
It may just be
that deception implores.
For those who have not
caught on to this yet
There's an old common term
to describe this old pest.
"The grass is greener"
are the words we all use.
Just wishing we were wearing
someone else's shoes.
Well, count all your blessings,
believe in your life.
Be gracious and satisfied
that you are alive.
Always remember,
for you are the star,
And you will be happy
right where you are.

I M P R I N T S

Why do we think,
The thoughts that we do?
Because the results of our past
Are what shape me and you.
The imprints once laid
Are so intertwined,
Our instinct and faith
Often follow behind.
Think about this:
The moment right now,
Forever takes part
in your future somehow.
If this is the case,
it's all worth the time,
To live every day
Like it's the end of the line.
Fulfill all your steps
Every second,
To mold a bright future
And a beautiful present.

INVESTING

How is the market?
We all need to know.
Checking it daily,
its highs and its lows.
No shortage of experts
on where it will lead.
Filling our heads
with fear and with greed.
We all know the mantra,
"Buy low and sell high."
Yet it turns so confusing
in the blink of an eye.
Emotions creep in there,
and what we once knew
Fights with our senses
and changes our view.
We measure in minutes
instead of by years,
And expect our decisions
to keep us in gear.
We think what we're doing
feels right in our heart,
But the world and its markets
can tear us apart.

Investing takes patience,
and knowledge and will.
And a constant commitment
to the plan that you build.
It's truly ironic
learning how to invest;
Doing the contrary
is often what's best.
When you look to the markets
and see doubt and despair
It's there you determine
if you succeed or you fail.
Getting out; filled with logic,
but it's often so wrong
You've got to get through it.
You've got to be strong.
So many graduates
not a day spent in class
Doing no homework
and expecting to pass.
Don't start with the where
until you learn how
The biggest mistake on the
amateur's brow.

I R O N Y

Life can be so confusing sometimes.
We must give to receive
Fail to succeed
Sacrifice to gain
And take on others' pain.
We must first learn to teach
Listen to be heard
Be poor in the spirit to be rich in the word.
We must live in the darkness
To know of the light
Let go to get back
If it's meant to be right.
We must trust when it's risky
Be patient for reward
Love when we needn't
Take the path which is hard.
We must share our abundance
Know that more is really less
Work when we're tired and pray for the best.
We must do unto others
And have faith we can't see
When we're plumb full of questions
We have to believe.
These are the secrets, the rules of our road
For those who live by them, a blessed abode.

IT'S TIME

Look at your watch
Tell me what you see;
Are you late for a meeting,
Do you wish you were free?
Coming and going,
not a second to lose
We're all on a mission
and there's so much to do.
What if there was thrown
a wrench in your gears,
What used to take minutes
now will take years!
In that moment of truth
Could you stand up and say,
"I'd do nothing different,
So glad for each day!"
Your free will is calling
The choice is for you,
Measure either by blessings
or tasks left to do.
Now regain your focus
to that watch on your wrist:
What's more important,
Your path or a list?
It's never too late
To stop on that road,
And help those who need it;
Lighten their load.
Time will move quickly
if you let it slide,
But to harness its beauty,
you'll look back with pride.

M E

Have you ever sat down
And thought about what you love?
I love freedom! And learning.
Great music adds to any occasion.
I love the world God created.
It could never be duplicated.
Friendship is up there.
Every friend you have in life is unique.
Positive energy with someone
can completely control you.
Relaxing in nature, another love of mine.
Business intrigues me.
It makes me think.
Quiet time alone:
That's where I build and grow.
Sharing with family—
I'm blessed to have a great one.
Giving to people.
Life is all connected.
You can't beat the simple life.
It builds character.
I love reality. It's so hard to face sometimes.
Interesting conversation is a plus.
I love success. Define it how you want.
How about the thought
of being bound to someone's soul.
I love knowing,
Tomorrow brings an uncertain certainty.
Who could forget … Dreaming
Dreams are what help you believe
anything is possible.
Everyone loves something in this world.
What do you love?

THE MEDAL

One day, three young boys were walking along the lake, just south of town. As they approached the old fishing dock, they noticed a paper sack. Upon closer examination, they saw that it was filled with money. The boys' hearts raced with emotion. After much argument, they decided to turn it in. If no one claimed it, then they would keep it.

As they returned to town, they ran into a homeless man. "Old man Tucker" they called him. He had never been right since his return from Vietnam, and had always lived outside, even in the winter. The children in town were warned to stay away from him. He approached and said hello. They nodded, somewhat fearfully. He proceeded to tell them about his life, and how he had watched them grow up. He said he'd been born in their small town, and that he knew that most of the adults were afraid of him. He said he knew he didn't look good, but he hoped they could be friends. Just then, he reached into his pocket and pulled out a star-shaped gold medal with a red, white, and blue ribbon. He said that this was the first time in years that anyone had listened to him, and he wanted the young boys to have it. He thanked them for their time and went on his way.

That afternoon, one of the boys told the story of the money and the man to his dad, who immediately recognized it as the Silver Star because his own father had earned one in World War II. He explained that Old man Tucker had earned it for gallantry in action against an armed enemy of the United States. The boys were mesmerized. As they walked outside to further admire the medal, the father yelled out, "Hey, what about this money?" One of the boys simply said, with little interest, "Let us know if anyone claims it."

A few weeks later, after learning much more war history, the boys ran into that old homeless man. As he approached and said hello, the boys again froze. And then, hesitantly, one of them stepped forward and said, "Sir, welcome home."

MEDIOCRE

Regular, standard, run of the mill,
Average, typical, never a thrill.
Right in the center
The bell curve will show,
What comfort it brings
There are still some below.
If there weren't a middle, there would not be a top,
That's true, but the thing is, our standards have dropped.
This culture we live in is shocking to see,
It's all how you feel, and don't blame it on me.
To measure advancement
It's you against you,
Not studies, not theories
Not poise-building tools.
There's winning and losing
Life will bring both,
If you want to build character
Know that loss turns to growth.
Do not let them fool you or detour your life's quest,
You were put on this earth to show us your best.
So, shine on like a diamond
Let your spirit take lead,
And make your life story a wonder to read.

NOBILITY

Back in the centuries
it was said of your worth,
Your rank was awarded
or given by birth.
Noble were great men
by title and course,
Leading the masses,
exalted by force.
So this got me thinking:
In our world, today
What makes a man noble?
Which light leads his way?
For some, it's important
from where you have come;
But to think this is noble
is a thought I'm far from.
To fight for somebody
whose voice can't be heard,
Or suffer for others
and not say a word.
To know you are winning,
yet choose to stand down;
To do what you can
for the poor in your town.
To step in the fire
for those you don't know,
To give when you've nothing

Bread for the Journey

To help someone grow.
Noble, to me, means
doing things others don't,
Having will and commitment
to change things others won't.
For all of you out there
(you know who you are),
I just want to thank you
We're better—by far.
In centuries forward
Of what will they make,
When they speak of the noble
And what part will you take?

RICH OR POOR

Will you look at those people
It's disgusting, I say
If we were in their shoes, could we live life that way?
What type of an image is stuck in your head?
A dirty man begging
Or a wealthy man's bread?
Why are we divided?
Let's focus instead
On what we've in common;
We'll all be ahead.
They say life brings duties
What duties are they?
To be self-sufficient or tithe along the way?
And what of our peoples
Whose life has been hard?
For those least among us do we just disregard?
There will be a season when you're asked to give
It won't be your money,
But how you have lived.
An honest accounting of each of your days
Will make worldly worries seem so far away.
Be not troubled of others and what they should do
Just live with your heart
And always be true.

T R U T H

How do you know when the things that you see
Are made of the truth stamped with "pure guarantee?"
Do you base it on knowledge
Or confide in a friend?
Is it just how you see it?
Can you simply pretend?
How pure and how simple can the truth even be?
Are there not many versions—one for you, one for me?
Sometimes I wonder if it isn't the case
That we're losing the structure of our truth and its place.
Truth is not feelings, nor opinion, nor want
And it does not depend on one's relative vaunt.
We may, as a people do without many things
To survive with no maxim
Should disaster it bring.
While not easy to speak to
Just look and you'll see
When truth shows its presence, the signs there will be.
It is built on decision
Through history and creed
With facts of precision
And of challenge no need.
It's not always easy to believe or agree
But one thing is for certain:
It will set you free.

THE UNCLEAN STONE (125 A.D.)

One day a young boy—dirty, barefoot, and poor—was walking
Down a long gravel road in the hot summer sun. He came upon
Some men who seemed to be upset, and were throwing rocks
Into a nearby lake. He recognized the men, whom his father had
Often spoken of, but had never spoken to. They were wealthy but
Unseemly local land owners, with nice clothing and new sandals.
The curious child went up to the men and asked what was the
Matter, and if he could help them one of the men angrily said to
Him, "We are throwing these filthy stones at the world. Our business
Has been taken over by men wealthier than ourselves, and we
Have been run out of town. Please leave us." The boy looked
At the pile of stones the men were throwing, picked one up,
And put it in his pocket. Later on that evening, the boy was
Examining his unique stone, and decided to tell his father the story.
The father was angry about his son talking to the men. And as he
Looked at his son's new rock, he realized it was simply coal. He
Told his son to never talk to the men again and threw the coal to
The ground. As it split into pieces, a large and beautiful diamond
Appeared. He looked at his son with amazement as tears came to
His eyes. He said, "My son, my son, you have given us riches."
The boy replied, "Father, I don't understand. If this stone contains
Riches as you say, why were those men throwing many riches
Into the lake?" The father hugged his son and replied, "Just a
Moment ago I was trying to teach you a lesson out of anger. Yet, it
Turns out that you, my young son, have provided me with a lifetime
Of lessons through the simple cast of an unclean stone.

"WALK A MILE IN YOUR SHOES"

It has long been said that in order to really understand someone, you must walk a mile in their shoes. This is timeless advice upon which we can all agree, and following it can help us to regard other with sympathy and patience. Well, how about this—have you ever thought about what someone's experience would be if they had to walk a mile in *your* shoes?

We spend our lives building perceptions, which are influenced by those around us, our culture, and what we choose to learn. So if someone had to live as you for a week, what would they think? Would they understand all that concerns you? Would you be comfortable with someone else knowing who you really are? Do you think your perceptions are accurate?

At any time, we can take inventory of who we truly are. Through this process, incredible things can be learned. We can never change unfair perceptions, nor should we. It's not what others think about us that's important, but what we personally understand about ourselves. Walking a mile in someone else's shoes can bring a great sense of understanding. Walking a mile in your own just may prevent you from having to wear so many pairs of other people's shoes.

See you on the trails!

WOUNDED

For those who are hurting, this one is for you:
The world is unfair and can even be cruel.
You sit back and wonder, "This pain that I feel
How can I fix it? The wound just won't heal."
We all have our seasons. The road seems so long
How will we get through it? We have to be strong.
This short time we're given, and the cards that we're dealt
Contain hidden blessings, a true kind of help.
But how do we focus when we can't see light
The burden's increasing and we don't want to fight.
Control what you're able; give it your best
There's always tomorrow for life's other requests.
Search for those good things that only you possess
Practice and build them and let time do the rest.
One day, unexpected, the sun will appear
Your heart will be lighter and your head will be clear.
For now, in this moment, so much left to do
Know this, my good friend:
I'll be praying for you.

YOU JUST DON'T KNOW

On a hot summer morning, old Joseph was late
For a big business meeting; his career it could make.
Traffic was stopped and his cell phone was dead
With his engine light blinking, he lowered his head.
"Why Lord, this morning, couldn't you see
How important this day is for my family and me?"
When he got home that evening he was met by his wife
His eyes, they explained it, the worst day of his life.
She told him to follow, and turned to the house
Saying, "We will get through this, I haven't a doubt."
Later that evening the boss gave a call
To check on Joe's safety—the fire'n all.
Joe had tried to reach them; he knew much too late
But they hadn't called back. He assumed they're irate.
Turns out that the meeting which caused so much strife
If he just would have made it, it'd taken his life.
It was going on midnight as Joe lay in bed,
Now in perspective were the words his wife said.
For just at that moment into his ear
The Lord softly whispered, "I heard loud and clear."

YOUR PLACE

The world is big, and we are small.
Why does it often seem like we are big and the world is small?
Maybe both are true.

The Earth has the power to destroy us,
Yet we have the power to destroy it.
One person in this world is so small
But each of our lives is so uniquely important.
The Earth spans thousands of miles,
but we are all connected.

We only meet a small number of people throughout our lives.
Yet a tiny breakthrough from just one of us
can change the course of human history for all of us.
Sometimes the world can seem to dictate our every move.
At the same time, we truly control our own personal destiny.
We come from differing cultures, backgrounds, and testimonies,
but somehow share the same common human desires.

At the beginning of our lives in this world,
it seems like time takes forever.
At the end of a life well lived, we wonder where the time went.
We invent technology, which expands our world in every direction.
At the end of the day, a book and a candle is all we need.
We cannot live without the world, and in turn,
the world cannot survive without us.

What is your place in this world?

Cornerstones for a Healthy Life

Cornerstones for a healthy life, part I

NEVER forget those who helped you succeed. Put yourself in a positive environment. Maintain balance in your life. Find your creativity and develop it fully. Don't be afraid to fail. Read a lot (library cards are free). Be interested in others. Take responsibility for your actions. Set your standards high. Focus on what you have, not what you don't. Be concerned about what you can control. Give…Even when no one is looking. Exercise. Be loyal to your friends. Help those who have less than you. Seek to understand.

Forgive and forget. Just when it's time to quit, go a little more. Do something no one has ever done before. Think. Love with all your heart. Be optimistic. Thank your creator for every day.

Cornerstones for a healthy life, part II

BE someone's door to success. It may be longer, but take the high road. Give without expectation

Show your "fiery" qualities. Do the hard thing. Make promises and keep them. Don't compete, change the game. Talk to someone you normally wouldn't. See things before they develop. Teach someone to read. Give you — what you need. Change when you don't have to. Be a capitalist. Goals limit, make dreams come true. Live in the now. Speak out for people who can't. Tell someone your great idea. Do stuff alone sometimes. Understand — skills vs qualities. Live beneath your means. Give away something you value much. Ask your mentors about their failures. Develop a solid decision making process. Embrace life's uncertain certainty. Stand tall, you have much to be proud of. Identify your fears and crush them. Know your spirit. Write your own history.

Cornerstones for a healthy life, part III

SMILE at the frowners in life. Make a budget and stick to it. Pave your own road to achievement. Enjoy your family, with all their faults. Risk it all when it feels right. Say you're sorry. Judge when it's appropriate. Allow good feelings to overwhelm you. Be consistently moving forward (the past is always close behind). Get involved in your community. Run through a cornfield. Don't make others wait for you. Express your opinions. Do things the fun way sometimes. Leave your comfort zone behind. Tell a child that you love them. Communicate effectively. Know that luck comes from preparation. Stretch your mind. Be counter intuitive (look it up). Visit the zoo once per year. Carry on meaningful traditions. Don't become what you own. Pray for the sick and dying. Make a solid first impression. Have your neighbors over for dinner. Shed from life what brings you down.

Cornerstones for a healthy life, part IV

HONOR that to which you are committed. Take great care of your own grass. Don't carry rocks in your pockets. Learn to manage ambiguity. Fish with a child who never has. Eat a huge piece of pie. Quit worrying about everything. Never stop building, no matter what. Make the time and do it. Assist someone you have never met. Learn how economics works. Clean out your closets, and throw. Know: the past belongs to history now. Create efficiency. Save your change…it adds up. Read the owner's manual for your car. Slow dance in your living room. Help restore someone's confidence. Seek the value in common sense. Change something you know is wrong. Walk to the store, like the old days. Focus on the holiday, not the day off. Put together a difficult puzzle. Make dinner at home for a whole month. Develop your memory (it can be done). Join a service organization. Write a "thank you" note to someone. Stretch your muscles every morning. Carry a friend when they need it. Understand cause and affect. Think of the other side of the argument. Write your life's mission statement. Diversify. Avoid traffic as much as possible. Spend a day with those who have nothing. Look up to the clouds and reflect. Bask in the freedom you have been given.

Cornerstones for a healthy life, part V

"LOOK OUT" for miracles. See the purpose, not the task. Plan... It works better. Don't look for bread where stones lie. Pay attention to the details. Develop your will, then will come skill. Put things into perspective. Make a life story to write about. Anticipate. Practice good manners. Get those old pictures in order. Plant a fruit tree. Address those thorny things in your life. Take pride in who you are right now. Know that each day adds to your legacy. Try a food you always hated... again. Listen. Stand firm in your faith. Do some serious manual labor. Create a better way to do something. Drink more tea. Spend that extra time with family. Find your own personal balance. Turn off the TV. Be a virtuous influence. Take one whole day to regroup. Give people more than they expect. Write a love letter. Conserve where you can. Let your instincts guide you. Serve those who are suffering. Focus on equality of the opportunity. Help someone just getting started. Dig into your mistakes and grow. Get some sleep. Roast more marshmallows by the fire. Have mercy. Sit and listen to some great old music. Call someone who lost their soul mate. Don't stop believin'.

Cornerstones for a healthy life, part VI

SHOW your character. Take the afternoon off sometimes. Give someone hope to carry on. Learn to survive in the woods. Make a plan to become debt free. Go without something. Let time heal that wound. Connect with an old friend. Review your valuable documents. Get a bird feeder. Research your beliefs. Write an article for the newspaper. Have a civil political discussion. Challenge your body. Make something from scratch. Ask an elder about childhood. Plan someone's retirement party. Watch an old movie. Thank a service person. Clean up after yourself. Take it to the next level. Say the Pledge of Allegiance. Always be respectful. Can some vegetables. Endure life's little inconveniences. Run with people smarter than you. Enjoy the weather…it's weather.. Be someone good to know. Cause change. Discover another language. Drink from the hose. Give a speech somewhere. Catch some fireflies. Stay home for a whole weekend. Never, never forget the poor. Rescue a puppy. Shine your shoes. Sit up straight. Look up your family tree. Vote. If it's not broken, break it. Go for that walk. Sharpen your time management. Volunteer (yes, you do have the time). Be a voice for you. Pick up worms after it rains. Get a really good massage. Read about history. Think about what you love. Be God's fingerprints. Shine on!

Cornerstones for a healthy life, part VII

DO random acts of kindness. Go for a walk when it's cold out. Don't look back in anger. Realize just how far you've come. Jump some rope. Learn about nutrition. Be comfortable standing alone. Cut costs before trouble starts. Go on a solitude retreat. Wax your car by hand. Volunteer at a hospice. Have a bonfire in the snow. Practice gratefulness. Attend your city council meeting. Be a "daydream believer". Simplify your life. Keep time in context. Have a neighborhood party. Volunteer in a political campaign. Get those home projects done. Gather your friends and serve a meal at a homeless shelter. Count your blessings before you have to. Attempt something you think is impossible right now. Babysit for new parents. Thank a fire fighter for their selfless dedication. Speak out for yourself even if your knees buckle. Send your parents flowers on <u>your</u> birthday. Know that angels are working overtime for you right now. Quit doing optional things which don't make your life better.

Cornerstones for a healthy life, part VIII

TAKE a train somewhere. Ask Dad what it used to be like (while you still can). Get out of your comfort zone. Fill those bike tires and use them. Start your own business. Choose to be happy and thankful. Pull the weeds in your life. Go to your hometown county fair. Seek to understand "wellness". Sit down at the table for dinner. Pick your children over technology. Know nothing good comes from fear. Work LESS. Family MORE. Write some poetry. Think about whose life you affect. Put a flag in your yard. Slow down. Use your picnic basket. Help some kids catch frogs. Embrace life transitions. Quit worrying about it. Take a day to plan your next year. Become an expert at something (besides your work). Finish your house projects. Have an old fashioned party. Give a little more to charity...more. Make some spaghetti sauce. Go see the leaves changing color. Hang out with friends from church. Enroll in a nature class. Help someone close who needs you. Eat tons and tons of veggies. Engage even when it's stressful. Define what your values are. Look for grace; it's everywhere.

www.ingramcontent.com/pod-product-compliance
Lightning Source LLC
Chambersburg PA
CBHW051845090426
42811CB00034B/2222/J